THE POWER
OF HIS REIGN

AN EASY INTRODUCTION
TO AMILLENNIALISM

Jonathan Ammon

The Power of His Reign by Jonathan Ammon
Published by Lowerlight Books

Cover Design by Hector Cortes

For Tatiana

CONTENTS

Contents

Acknowledgments

This book owes a great debt to the hard work of teaching and searching the Scriptures that others have done. I did not come up with amillennialism or the core concepts presented in this book. I became fascinated as I pored over the work of scholars like Anthony Hoekema and Sam Storms. As the introduction describes, I did not set out to write a book. I simply devoured seminary lectures, books, and articles on the topic of eschatology. When it came time to set down what I learned, I pulled from the mix of knowledge and wisdom I had accumulated from my own study of the Scriptures and what I had been taught through hours of material. I have done my best to cite anyone who I have paraphrased or quoted, and to include a bibliography of each lecture and work that was part of my study of eschatology in the last two years. The greatest acknowledgment must go to Dr. Sam Waldron. Dr. Waldron and I would disagree about a great many matters, but his material on eschatology has been the most helpful in my own study. This book has been greatly influenced by his work.

I also must thank Jim McKnight who believed that it was important for the leaders he was training to know what they believed about the end times and spurred on the study that led to this book.

INTRODUCTION

I grew up believing that Christ was going to return. I was taught that Christ would rapture the church before a seven-year tribulation, that there were different judgments for the wicked and the righteous, and that Christ would reign on the earth for a thousand years before the battle of Armageddon. This is what I now know is called dispensational premillennialism.

The details are fuzzy in my mind, and most of what I remember from this time is the rapture and the popularity of the *Left Behind* books. I was radically born again at seventeen and immediately read the Bible cover to cover a few times. I couldn't find the rapture anywhere. I couldn't find multiple judgments anywhere either.

The judgment seat of Christ was something I thought about a lot in those years, and I became certain that there was no secret rapture of the church or a separate judgment for believers at a different time than unbelievers. I had no idea how much these simple ideas should have impacted the rest of my views on the end times.

I continued to devour the Word of God and felt certain that I should understand as much as possible about all that the Bible had to teach. I came to believe that the church of Jesus Christ would indeed go through the tribulation and that Christ would return before a millennial reign on the earth, what's called a post-tribulation premillennial view. I came to this view through teaching by Dr. Michael Brown, Mike Bickle, and Zac Poonen whose sermon series on Israel and the book of Revelation I studied multiple times. ==However, I also became more and more frustrated with believers who were obsessed with the end times.==

The popularity of the *Left Behind* books had diminished, but I still ran into believers who were far more excited about end times prophecy than they were about the Great Commission. This frustrated me, and in response I tabled much of my pursuit of understanding the different views about the end times and simply read Revelation as a book about worshipping Christ and spiritual warfare. This season was immensely edifying. I still struggle with believers who are obsessed with Bible prophecy or want to press controversial theological views about the end times on others.

==This book won't be like that. My hope is that it will be a simple and practical introduction to one biblical view of the end times.== I am not bitter with those who taught me their end times views. I don't believe that those who disagree with me about the end times are deceived by Satan. I simply believe that what I present in this book is the clearest biblical teaching I can give on the end times.

In the midst of conversation with some other friends and ministers who shared my views I ended up confessing that I didn't understand logically how a millennial kingdom on earth after the return of Christ fit with what was written in 1 Corinthians 15 or 2 Peter 3. My friends, who had received degrees from a Bible college and held credentials with a denomination that had premillennialism in its statement of faith, agreed. But we were all premillennial, and so were all the teachers we respected.

A few years ago, my mentor mentioned offhand that he was amillennial—that he didn't believe that Jesus was going to physically reign on the earth before the New Heavens and the New Earth. This was the first time I had ever met someone who held this view, and I realized I didn't know anything about amillennialism. I couldn't articulate the arguments or position of amillennialism, and while I

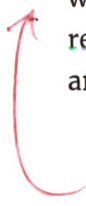

Amazing

2

had grappled with postmillennialism and preterism a little, I had no knowledge of amillennialism at all. I decided to investigate amillennialism for myself.

I searched for free seminary course lectures on amillennialism and found Covenant Baptist Theological Seminary's course on eschatology by Dr. Sam Waldron. I was immediately fascinated. I ended up listening to the whole course multiple times, auditing two more seminary courses on amillennialism and reading several books on the subject.

Amillennialism was so simple. It was so biblical. This view took everything the Bible said at face value and could be understood by any believer. Why had I never heard this taught? Why were 90% of the books on the end times about premillennialism?

I wanted to let everyone know about the amillennial view. But I had trouble finding a way to do that. There are several good books about amillennialism, but virtually all of them are scholarly and from a reformed perspective. I wanted something simple and introductory that I could recommend to anybody. I wanted something to give to my charismatic and Arminian friends. I wanted something I could give to those who would never pick up an academic text.

When I couldn't find that book, I decided to try to write one myself. I am not a scholar or a theologian. This is not an academic or scholarly work. This book is by no means a complete look at the end times. This is a simple and positive introduction to the basic framework of amillennialism that I hope anyone can read.

This book is just an introduction; you should go to the Scriptures and the excellent scholarly works I mention to learn more about amillennialism and the end times. What's more you should go to the Holy Spirit, who Jesus promises will tell us about things that are to come.

CHAPTER 1: INTRODUCING AMILLENNIALISM

"The time is fulfilled, and the kingdom of God is at hand; repent and believe in the gospel." Mark 1:15b

W hen Jesus launched into ministry after His baptism, He proclaimed a radical message: the kingdom of God is here! It's time to stop living for ourselves—in unbelief and doubt of God's love and power—and turn to Him in full trust and obedience. Christ's ministry continues. Today He is spreading His reign and the kingdom of God throughout the earth using His church. This is the message of amillennialism. Christ is reigning now, and He will use His church to spread His reign through the earth until His return.

We can look forward to the kingdom of God growing even as deception grows in the world. God allows His Kingdom to grow like wheat in a field full of weeds. Human hearts will grow harder. Their love will grow colder, but those who love Christ will stay faithful until the end. The great story of spiritual warfare will climax in history as Satan will finally be allowed to deceive the nations on a global scale. What Satan sought to do through the kingdoms of the world from the first century until now through rulers like Nero, Stalin, Hitler, and others will finally be accomplished in one last antichrist. The nations of the world will war against the church.

In this dark hour Christ will return as a victor drenched in blood. He will raise the dead in Christ, conquer His enemies and bring small and great, dead and living, before the judgment seat of Christ. This resurrection of the dead will mean the end of physical death forever. Human beings will no longer be subject to the decay of their physical bodies as each individual is raised to stand before Christ.

This final judgment will include all men. Christ will sort the righteous from the unrighteous, the faithful from the wicked. Those who love Christ and His name will enter into eternal life. Those who reject Christ will be cast into the lake of fire prepared for the devil and his servants.

The earth as we know it will be destroyed with fire as God brings about a New Heaven and New Earth where the two are joined together rather than separated. We will experience the light of the glory of God in the New Jerusalem. There will be no more death and no more tears. All of our relationships to one another will be perfected—so much so that even marriage will become obsolete. Only the righteous and only righteousness will live in that place.

This is the message of amillennialism. That Christ's reign and kingdom is right now. That Satan will deceive the nations before the end of time, but that Christ will return in glory to conquer His enemies, raise the dead, and the judge all of humanity. This earth will be destroyed by fire, and we will live with Christ in the New Jerusalem and the New Heavens and New Earth. We will explore these concepts in the Scriptures through the rest of this book.

which has already come — in its first fruits.

There are different views within amillennialism. Some are more optimistic about the end times and don't believe in an antichrist figure, a tribulation, or a final battle. Some disagree on what the details of what Christ's reign means. Others have a highly developed view of the tribulation and the antichrist. But all amillennialists agree that Christ is reigning on the earth today through His church. We don't look forward to a future kingdom on earth where Christ reigns in physical form before the resurrection. We look forward to Christ's return, the resurrection of the dead, and our entrance into the age to come and the eternal state. In that eternal state Christ will physically reign on the New Earth and fulfill the many prophecies of transformed life on earth under His reign.

Unlike dispensational premillennialism, amillennialism is not a system that has a place for every verse in the Bible. It provides a clear way of understanding the general biblical teaching on the end times but allows for many beliefs about the details of what will occur at the end. This book will leave some with more questions, as amillennialism in general allows for multiple views about the tribulation, the antichrist, or the interpretation of biblical prophecy. I hope that this will motivate you to read the Scriptures in a fresh light and move on to deeper studies of the subject.

Amillennialism is simple. So simple in contrast to some end times theology that it can take time to adjust. Can understanding the end times really be that easy? I believe that the Bible's message about the end is really that simple. God gives us many pictures—many visions—of the end, but each one is consistent with this simple message about our hope in the present kingdom of God and the coming of Jesus Christ our Lord.

We will introduce amillennialism again in the next chapter and then show it side by side with the other major views of the end times in Chapter 2. This chapter will introduce some theological terms and systems. Stick with it. These terms don't mean that things have to be complicated. You can always look back through the book to remind yourself what something means.

After introducing the major views, we will examine how we approach the Scriptures so we can understand why believers are so divided on this issue, and why I believe the end times can be so simple. And then we will move through the Bible's clearest passages about the end, revealing the biblical message piece by piece and building an elegant portrait of our blessed hope and the return of our Master Jesus Christ in glory.

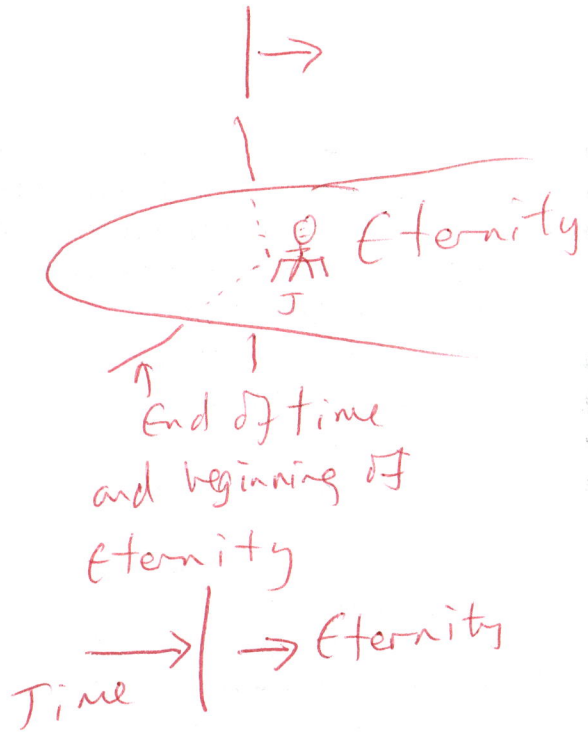

CHAPTER 2: MAJOR END TIME VIEWS

He brought up eschatology in the first five minutes of the conversation." God told my friends Bud and Denise about His plan to awaken the church and raise up an end times army, and they are doing it.[1] They participate in movements of churches planting churches across the U.S. and the globe. They also travel around the United States praying for churches. When I asked them how it was going, they told many encouraging stories, but also one story of a pastor who immediately wanted to know their stance on the end times.

The end times are controversial. Ministries, churches, and denominations draw boundaries based on end times beliefs. While I want to inform you of what I believe is the most biblical interpretation of the end times message, I don't want to be a bully or put too much emphasis on issues that divide us. I am most certain of the core truth of the gospel and who Jesus is. The further we get from that core, the less certainty I have about any topic. I believe this is right and good. While I believe that we can know the simple truth about what the Bible teaches about the end, I am by no means as certain of this teaching as I am about my experience with Jesus or

---

[1] Check out www.tenminas.net.

the gospel, and I hope to be gracious with those who believe differently than I do in this area.

In this first chapter I will lay out the major views held by Christians concerning the end times. I will attempt to be brief and fair, and I will try to raise many of the major questions about what will happen at the apocalypse and the end of this world. Many of the issues I raise in this chapter will be addressed in later chapters as we go through what the Bible says about the end times passage by passage.

An Eschatological Overview

The major views about the end times have been divided according to how they interpret Revelation 20:1-10. Starting your study on the end times with one of the last chapters in a highly symbolic apocalyptic book is not the best approach. But if we want to summarize the major views we must start here. The next chapter presents what I believe is the best way to approach interpreting the Bible and the passages about the end times. I believe it is best to start with the Bible's straight-forward passages and then use what we learn from the Bible's clear teaching to interpret more difficult passages like Revelation 20.

Because the study of last things, eschatology, has divided into separate views according to the interpretation of Revelation Chapter 20:1-10, we must be familiar with the text in order for those views to make sense.

Then I saw an angel coming down from heaven, holding in his hand the key to the bottomless pit and a great chain. 2 And he seized the dragon, that ancient serpent, who is the devil and Satan, and bound him for a thousand years, 3 and threw him into the pit, and shut it and sealed it over him, so that he might not deceive the nations any longer, until the thousand years were ended. After that he must be released for a little while.

4 Then I saw thrones, and seated on them were those to whom the authority to judge was committed. Also I saw the souls of those who had been beheaded for the testimony of Jesus and for the word of God, and those who had not worshiped the beast or its image and had not received its mark on their foreheads or their hands. They came to life and reigned with Christ for a thousand years. 5 The rest of the dead did not come to life until the thousand years were ended. This is the first resurrection. 6 Blessed and holy is the one who shares in the first resurrection! Over such the second death has no power, but they will be priests of God and of Christ, and they will reign with him for a thousand years.

7 And when the thousand years are ended, Satan will be released from his prison 8 and will come out to deceive the nations that are at the four corners of the earth, Gog and Magog, to gather them for battle; their number is like the sand of the sea. 9 And they marched up over the broad plain of the earth and surrounded the camp of the saints and the beloved city, but fire came down from heaven and consumed them, 10 and the devil who had deceived them was thrown into the lake of fire and sulfur where the beast and the false prophet were, and they will be tormented day and night forever and ever. (Revelation 20:1-10) ESV

JC rtns before a literal 1000 yr reign

Premillennialism

Premillennialism states that Christ is going to come back before a future millennium and that during that future millennium Christ is going to physically reign on the earth for 1,000 years. At the end of that 1,000 years, the evil men who exist on the earth will attack the people of God.

There are multiple views within premillennialism.

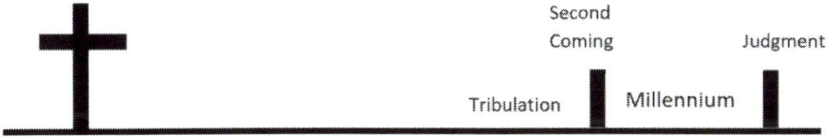

Post-tribulational Premillennialism states that the tribulation (a time of judgment and disaster before the end described in several passages and often identified with Revelation 6-9 and 16) will occur followed by the second coming of Christ. Christ will then physically

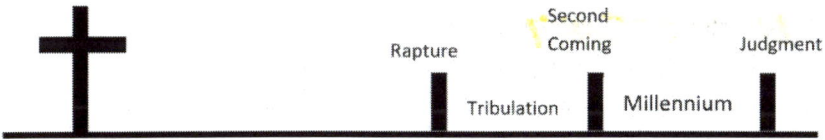

reign on the earth for 1,000 years followed by the final judgment.[2]

Pre-tribulational   Premillennialism   or   Dispensational Premillennialism states that Christ will return to rapture the church. This will be followed by the tribulation. After the tribulation, Christ will return with the resurrected Church and physically reign on the earth for 1000 years before the resurrection of the wicked and the final judgment of unbelievers.

The **Mid-Tribulation** view states that Christ will return at the seventh trumpet (Revelation 11:15-19) which they identify as the last trumpet in 1 Corinthians 15:52 and 1 Thessalonians 4:16. This view posits that Christ will return after the seven trumpets but before the bowls of wrath are poured out upon the earth in Revelation 16. Mid-Tribulation proponents argue that Jesus died on the cross and took

---

[2] All of the graphics in this book were inspired by
Lamorak. (2010). Comparison of Christian millennial interpretations [Online image]. Retrieved from URL (https://upload.wikimedia.org/wikipedia/commons/8/89/Millennial_views.svg)

God's wrath for the church. The church will never have to endure God's wrath again, therefore the church cannot be present for the pouring out of the bowls of wrath.

after a literal 1000 yr reign

Postmillennialism

Postmillennialism asserts that Christ will return after the 1000-year rule upon the earth. This 1000-year period represents the success of the church's mission on the earth.

There are two different approaches within postmillennialism.

The **Revivalist** approach states that the 1000-year reign of Christ represents a time of Christian revival and success in mission that will then usher in the return of Christ.

The **Reconstructionist** approach states that the church's success in mission will result in a theocratic rule. They believe Christians will rule the earth for a literal or figurative 1000-year reign that will usher in the return of Christ.

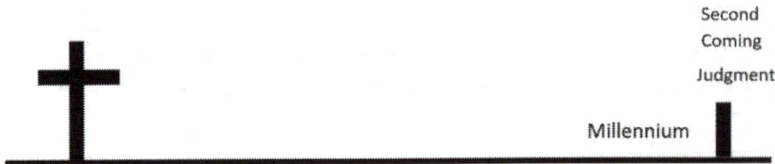

Second
Coming

Judgment

Millennium

The postmillennial timeline would see the church age continuing until a point when the church's mission becomes a success, or the majority of the world is Christian. That success will last for the Millennium, after which humanity will briefly rebel leading into the second coming and the final judgment. There are different views on what will ultimately bring about the Millennium in postmillennialism, but it will be the victory of the church.

Amillennialism

Amillennialism states that we are currently in the 1,000-year rule of Christ in Revelation 20:1-10. The 1000-year reign represents the

current reign of Christ over his church and the kingdom of God or the present reign of deceased Saints with Christ.

There are two views within amillennialism.

Optimistic Amillennialism is similar to revival postmillennialism. It asserts that key events of the tribulation have already occurred and that the church will see an increase in the success of mission before the return of Christ.

Pessimistic Amillennialism suggests that the state of the world will worsen or escalate into the tribulation or that though the church's success in mission increases, the world's wickedness also increases.

The amillennialism timeline shows that we are currently in the symbolic millennial reign of Christ and that the second coming and the final judgment will occur in rapid succession in the future.

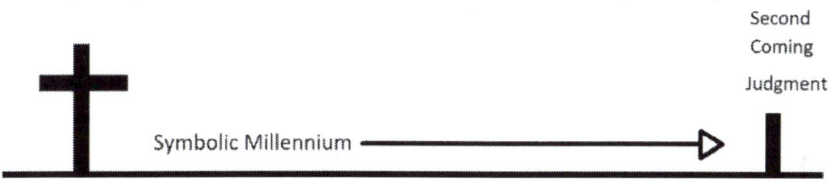

Symbolic Millennium ⟶ Second Coming / Judgment

Interpreting Biblical Prophecy

Along with these millennial views there are multiple ways to interpret biblical prophecy. How should we handle the prophetic passages in the Book of Daniel or in the Book of Revelation or in Matthew 24?

Preterism

Preterism posits that most or many biblical prophecies regarding the end times were fulfilled in 70 AD. Preterism relies on the book of Revelation being written before 70 AD. **Partial Preterism** states that many or most prophecies were fulfilled in 70 AD but that we still look forward to Christ's bodily return and the resurrection of our bodies.

Full Preterism or hyper preterism states that all end time prophecies were fulfilled in 70 AD, that Christ has already returned, the new heavens and the new earth have already been established, and that there is no physical resurrection. For most of Christian history full preterism has been considered a heresy, though it is more popular now than it has ever been.

What Happened in 70AD?

In 70AD the Jews in Judea rebelled against the roman Empire. Emperor Nero sent the Roman army to put down the rebellion. They slaughtered the Jews, defiled the holy place, and completely destroyed the Temple, not leaving one stone upon another. While Jesus put an end to the sacrificial system for believers through the death on the cross, the destruction of the temple put a literal end to the sacrificial system for the Jews as the law required that sacrifices be made in the temple.

Futurism

This is the view most of us grew up with. Futurism states that many or most end times prophecies have a future fulfillment. Most of the book Revelation, and key prophecies in Daniel, and Matthew 24 will come to pass in the future.

Historicism

Historicism argues that most end times prophecy has a historical fulfillment from 70 AD and beyond, through the second and third century.

Idealism

Idealism states that many or most of these biblical prophecies have an ongoing fulfillment because they are symbolic of a spiritual reality. They teach us truths about spiritual warfare and patterns of demonic and spiritual activity in the heavenly places as well as on *all* earth.

More Questions

Multiple Returns, Resurrections, Judgments?
    Another issue for debate: Are there multiple returns of Christ? Is Christ going to return for his church and then return again at the end for judgment? Or will he return once to do both?

Are there multiple resurrections? Is Christ going to resurrect the Saints first and then a thousand years later resurrect unbelievers? Or is there only one resurrection of the dead that includes both believers and unbelievers?

Judgments?
    Are there multiple judgments? Is there a separate judgment where believers get rewards? Or will believers be part of the final judgment where they are judged according to their deeds?

Timing and Sequence?
    The timing and sequence of the return of Christ, the judgment, the destruction of this earth and the arrival of the new heavens and the new earth are debated. Do all of these occur at the same time or are there long periods of time between them?
    There are even more questions about the anti-Christ, the tribulation, the final battle before Christ returns, and more. This book won't answer all these questions, but I hope to give a clear introduction to each issue above.

Why does this matter? → *because what a person believes directly decides what that person does (= how he/ she, behaves = lives .).* 15

I promised this book would be simple, but you may be feeling overwhelmed and wondering why you need to figure all of these things out. Does understanding the end times really matter?

There are a number of ways we can apply the truths about the end times to our lives.

1. **What we believe about the end times affects our expectation.** Can we expect Christ to rescue us from this present trouble and that is he going to guard us from the apocalypse on the apocalyptic events at the end of the world? Or should we be expecting the church's mission to succeed and Christ's return to be a victory celebration as we overcome the earth? Or can we expect to have to endure even greater suffering as the world gets worse and worse?

2. **What we believe about the end times affects how closely we live to that reality.** What about the imminence of the return of Christ? Can we really expect Christ to return at any time? Could Christ return today or are we waiting for fulfillments of prophecy?

3. **What we believe about the end times affects our politics.** Does foreign policy toward Israel matter to the end times? Should we seek political success, or should we be is seeking to advance a theocratic or moral rule over the earth because God's promised us that in the thousand-year reign?

4. **What we believe about the end times will affect what we believe about Scripture.** Do we believe the Scriptures can be understood by everybody with the help of the Holy Spirit? Can we really understand what the scriptures say about the end times or will we never be able to get this right? Are those scriptures applicable for us today or do they describe something that's all happened entirely in the past?

What most excites me is that Jesus made the end times simpler than many realize. He clarified the end far beyond the Hebrew Scriptures. But before we dive into Jesus's teaching, let's provide the key to many difficult questions by outlining an approach to Scripture's teaching about the end.

CHAPTER 3: APPROACHING THE SCRIPTURE

W"e should read the Bible in a vacuum." I was leading a Bible study in college and was full of zeal. In my mind too many people were interpreting the Bible through their experience. My heart was in the right place, but since then I have had to acknowledge that reading the Bible in a vacuum is just not possible.

All of us approach the Scripture with presuppositions—assumptions and worldviews that we bring with us. These presuppositions inform and impact how we see and hear the truth. No one approaches the Bible in a vacuum. All of us approach the word of God with experiences and ideas—both true and false.

We want to hear the Holy Spirit through the word of God, and we want God to reveal His mind to us. The Scripture itself promises us that we have the mind of Christ (1 Cor 2:16), and that the Holy Spirit Himself will guide us into all truth (John 16:13). Peter, inspired by that same Spirit, wrote that the Scripture isn't of any private interpretation (2 Peter 1:20). What it says and what it means, it says and means for all. It doesn't mean something different for us than it did for the very first audience who heard it. Yet, miraculously, it remains relevant and applicable for all.

The body of Christ is led by the Spirit into all truth and possesses all truth. Yet heresy spreads through different parts of the church. Different denominations and faith traditions huddle around areas of disagreement in the body like predestination and foreknowledge, charismatic gifts, the baptism in the Holy Spirit, church government, infant baptism, and the end times. Clearly not all of us know all of the mind of Christ on every issue. Some of us are wrong.

While not all of us are false teachers, all of us are erroneous teachers. Not one of us is perfect in all that he or she says or teaches. All of us must contend with our presuppositions, our pride, our desire to justify ourselves, and many other attitudes touched by this fallen world. How can we approach the Word confidently when there are so many disagreements among so many brothers? Even more troubling, how can we be confident in how we approach the Scriptures about the end times, a subject immersed in controversy and varied interpretation of highly symbolic passages?

As with many areas of spiritual life, God has given us ways to remain accountable to the truth that help keep us safe and guide as we pursue revelation from the Holy Spirit in the Scriptures. These measures of accountability or disciplines of interpreting Scripture are called Hermeneutics. Hermeneutics is its own field of study, but I will go over some basics here because how we approach the Scriptures will determine how we understand what they say about the end times.

Scripture Interprets Scripture

One of the first things I was taught about understanding and interpreting Scripture was that "Scripture interprets Scripture." Also known as the "*analog fide*," this approach is held by most believers and presented by several creeds and confessions. As far as I know, I

19

have yet to meet a believer who would disagree with this statement in principle. We should use the Bible to interpret the Bible. We should cross reference Scripture and form doctrine by allow the teachings of the text stand next to one another and explain one another.

Though many agree that Scripture interprets Scripture, questions remain. How does Scripture interpret Scripture? Which Scriptures should interpret which Scriptures? When it comes to the end times, which passages should we look at first and prioritize?

The Clear before the Difficult

I believe that a sound approach to the Scriptures, especially where eschatology is concerned, prioritizes the clear teaching of Scripture before the difficult, and the plain passages before the symbolic. We should look at what the Bible clearly and indisputably says about the end times before we approach the more difficult and disputed passages. With this approach we can use what is clear and simple to help us understand the difficult and complex. Clear Scripture will interpret difficult Scripture.

In this book we will look at the teaching passages in the gospels and epistles first and use what we learn from those passages to help us interpret the more difficult passages in the epistles along with the prophetic, apocalyptic, and symbolic passages. I believe that this approach will reveal that what the Bible teaches about the end times is actually simple and easy to understand for every believer. These passages were not meant to be difficult but meant to hold meaning for God's people in every age and time. They are rich in truth that the Holy Spirit will apply to our lives.

Allow the New Testament to Interpret the Old Testament

The Old Testament Scriptures are the inspired and infallible word of God. They contain vast information about eschatology and the end times. However, much of the Old Testament Scriptures are enmeshed in a temple and law system that is only a shadow of the reality who is Christ (Col 2:17). The Old Covenant was a dark distorted image of glory when compared to the clarity and beauty of Jesus.

Many of the prophecies and passages about the Messiah were fulfilled in a far different way than was expected. In the same way, much of what the Old Testament says about the End Times will be fulfilled in ways that were not clear at the time the Old Testament Scriptures were written.

We should look at the New Testament as an inspired commentary on the Old Testament. We should carefully trace the New Testament author's use of the Old Testament and allow the New Testament Scriptures to interpret the Old Testament. Passages like Acts 1 and 2 should help us interpret end times passages in Ezekiel. The book of Revelation should help us interpret the book of Daniel. We should look at the Old Testament passages on eschatology through the lens of the New Testament rather than prioritizing Old Testament revelation on eschatology over what the New Testament teaches.

Literal and Symbolic

One of the first things I was taught about Scripture was that we should interpret it "literally." This became a catchphrase, so much so that I remember hearing it in a Christian Reggae song while I was a teenager. Even though I heard many people championing a "literal" approach to the Scripture, I now realize that most teachers who used this phrase did not mean that they always interpreted the Bible literally. They meant that they took what the Bible said seriously and believed in the supernatural. They did not overly spiritualize the text, robbing it of plain sense or of the miraculous.

The Bible contains a number of books of different genres. It features poetry and prophecy, visions and dreams, as well as plain teaching. The Bible uses metaphors over and over again, and it would be foolish to take all of these metaphors literally. In Song of Songs, the Scripture does not intend to teach that a woman's teeth are literally a flock of sheep. We easily recognize this as a metaphor. The Book of Daniel, Revelation, and a number of other passages in the Old Testament Prophets also contain numerous symbols and require interpretation. These books were intentionally written to be symbolic. God intended for there to be symbols in the text.

A famous dispensational writer claimed that taking the Bible and the book of Revelation literally was the key to understanding the end times. But his writing is full of symbolic interpretation. He claimed that the locusts in Revelation 9 are actually helicopters. He compared the shape of the locust with the shape of a specific type of helicopter and posits that the locusts mentioned in the text are in fact helicopters. But this is not a literal interpretation. A literal interpretation would be that the locusts are literally locusts.

I believe that both interpretations miss the mark. Instead, we should allow Scripture to interpret Scripture and look for what locusts meant and symbolized in other parts of the Bible. I admit that this is not a literal interpretation, but I do believe it is a faithful and true interpretation.

The book of Revelation was not meant to be a literal description of future events. It was a visual message about the end, containing symbols rich with meaning not only for the believers of that day (who would not have been aware of helicopters), but throughout history and into the present day. That is the power of the prophetic word and the potency of symbolic apocalyptic language.

Where do we Start?

Where we start our study on the end times and what passages we give priority will determine how we understand what the Bible says about the end. If we start with Revelation 20, read it literally and then press the rest of the Bible to fit that interpretation, we will ultimately arrive at premillennialism. But if we start with clear passages about

Very imp. statement

the end times that Jesus and the epistle writers set down as clear doctrine we will arrive at a different understanding.

This is where the difference between the views ultimately lies. Premillennialists will either argue that Revelation 20 is in fact a clear passage, or that regardless of clarity we must start with the Old Testament revelation and then fit what the New Testament teaches within its framework. All of the disagreements about the end times come down to how we approach the Scriptures.

In this book I am going to start with what I believe are Jesus's clearest and most important teachings about the end, and then move to didactic passages from the apostles like 2 Peter 3 and 1 Corinthians 15 before approaching more difficult passages like 2 Thessalonians 2 and Revelation 20. We will start with Jesus's teaching in Luke 20.

Jesus teaching
↓
letters
} *clear*
↓ *to*
confusing/unclear

the clear must interpret the unclear.

CHAPTER 4: JESUS' TEACHING: LUKE 20

What does the Bible say about cremation?" It was Thanksgiving, and we were getting ready to start dinner. My friends and I were discussing the resurrection of the dead. Most of us were cross-cultural workers and different cultures follow different burial customs according to what they believe about the resurrection. Muslims bury their loved ones within twenty-four hours of death and forbid cremation. Historically, Christians did not cremate either, but we know that God will raise all the dead on the last day. He can raise people from the dust.[3]

The Sadducees also had questions about the resurrection from the dead.

There came to him some Sadducees, those who deny that there is a resurrection, 28 and they asked him a question, saying, "Teacher, Moses wrote for us that if a man's brother dies, having a wife but no children, the man must take the widow and raise up offspring for his brother. 29 Now there were seven brothers. The first took a wife, and died without children. 30 And the second 31 and the third took her, and likewise all seven left no

---

[3] Or in Abraham's case from the ashes. See Hebrews 11:19.

children and died. 32 Afterward the woman also died. 33 In the resurrection, therefore, whose wife will the woman be? For the seven had her as wife."
(Luke 20:27-33) ESV

The Sadducees were a group of religious leaders who were convinced that there was no resurrection of the dead. They didn't think God was going to raise people's physical bodies at the end of time. The Sadducees came to question and try to trick Jesus. Why? Because Jesus clearly believed in the resurrection of the dead. We should also.

In an effort to trap Jesus, the Sadducees came up with what they thought was a tricky scenario. If the dead were raised, what happened to widowed women who remarried. Who would they be married to in heaven?

Jesus answered their question and boldly confronted their error. In the process Jesus, clearly and succinctly gave his followers a wealth of information about both heaven and the end times.

Jesus replied, "The people of this age marry and are given in marriage. 35 But those who are considered worthy of taking part in the age to come and in the resurrection from the dead will neither marry nor be given in marriage, 36 and they can no longer die; for they are like the angels. They are God's children, since they are children of the resurrection. 37 But in the account of the burning bush, even Moses showed that the dead rise, for he calls the Lord 'the God of Abraham, and the God of Isaac, and the God of Jacob.' 38 He is not the God of the dead, but of the living, for to him all are alive." (Luke 20:34-38) NIV

Jesus clarifies the end times, the resurrection, and the state of humanity by providing a simple system of teaching. He divides time and space into "this age," which refers to this present time and world and "the age to come," which refers to a future age or world (the Greek word *kosmos*). Jesus continued to teach about these two ages throughout the Scriptures, and the apostles continued the same line of teaching. Along with this division, Jesus divided people into two types, the type that belong to and exist in this world: "the sons of this age," and those that belong to the resurrection and the age to come which He pairs together in verse 35.

In the above passage Jesus clearly teaches a contrast between the two.

The sons of this age	In the resurrection and the age to come
Marry	There is no marriage
Die	There is no death
Mixture of worthy and unworthy	Only the worthy (sons of God) exist in that age
Natural men	Resurrected men

Clearly the "age to come" requires a supernatural transformation of human beings and the world. The resurrection of the dead will change everything. Before the resurrection we enjoy marriage. As unsettling as the thought may be, after the resurrection we no longer exist in covenants of marriage. Only supernatural transformation ends the covenant of marriage.

Before the resurrection we experience death. But after the resurrection, in the eternal state, we no longer experience death.

Before the resurrection a mixture of worthy and unworthy people exists together—both believers and unbelievers, sinners and saints. In the resurrection and the age to come, the judgment separates the godly and ungodly. Only the worthy—the sons of God—live in the age to come.

This world is full of natural men with natural bodies, but the age to come is full of resurrected men with resurrected bodies. The resurrection of the dead brings us into a new age where we live forever among the saints as a resurrected people.

This is simple and clear teaching from Jesus. It may seem too simple. You may think, "Of course, I've always believed that," or, "Yes, I knew this already." I hope so. That means you've read the Scriptures and taken them at face value. But the most popular system of eschatology disagrees with what I have written here.

Premillennialism asserts that *after* the resurrection but *before* the eternal state Jesus will reign on the earth and despite what is taught here that even after the resurrection of the dead there will be marriage. There will be a mixture of worthy and unworthy men (who revolt against Christ's earthly rule before the end). There will be death, and there will be natural men rather than resurrected men on the earth.

Clearly that teaching does not come from this passage. Premillennialists must reinterpret this passage in order to match their understanding of Revelation 20.

I believe this passage is clear, simple, and foundational for our view of the end times, and that Jesus' teaching here can be taken at face value. Christ reigns now, in this imperfect age, and He will reign in the age to come. The age to come will arrive on the Lord's day at the resurrection of the dead and the final judgment when Jesus will supernaturally transform the world and all marriage, mixture of worthy and unworthy, natural bodies, and death will be done away with. We live in this present age, yet we experience the hope and the power of the age to come. We will return to the two ages that Jesus taught in Luke 20, but in the next chapter we will examine some of the most hope filled passages about the end: Jesus's parables.

CHAPTER 5: JESUS'S END TIME PARABLES

W hat I'm about to share is what I think is the most effective vision casting I've ever done. Would someone like to read Matthew 13:31-32?" My friend Jim went on to share about the parable of the mustard seed, using questions to illuminate how God plans for the kingdom to expand and grow through the multiplication of disciples and churches. This is not an abstract idea for Jim. Jim is one of the leaders of a church planting network in the U.S. military that has seen many streams of fourth generation church and beyond (a church that plants a church that plants a church that plants a church).[4]

What Jim described, and what he is experiencing, is the fulfillment of Jesus's end time parables. They both inspire and instruct. They are simple but full of information. Many of Jesus's parables in Matthew 13 directly or indirectly touch on the same subjects as Luke 20 and Jesus's answer to the Sadducees about the resurrection and the age to come.

---

[4] See Noplaceleftarmy.net

> [24] He put another parable before them, saying, "The kingdom of heaven may be compared to a man who sowed good seed in his field, [25] but while his men were sleeping, his enemy came and sowed weeds among the wheat and went away. [26] So when the plants came up and bore grain, then the weeds appeared also. [27] And the servants of the master of the house came and said to him, 'Master, did you not sow good seed in your field? How then does it have weeds?' [28] He said to them, 'An enemy has done this.' So the servants said to him, 'Then do you want us to go and gather them?' [29] But he said, 'No, lest in gathering the weeds you root up the wheat along with them. [30] Let both grow together until the harvest, and at harvest time I will tell the reapers, "Gather the weeds first and bind them in bundles to be burned, but gather the wheat into my barn."'" (Matthew 13:24-30) ESV

In this parable Jesus compared the Kingdom of heaven to a man who sows good seed. Here the Kingdom arrives first as a time of seed-sowing followed by a time of harvest. Until the harvest the righteous and the wicked will both remain in the world as a mixture even though the Kingdom has arrived in one stage. This parable touches on the "now and not yet" themes of Jesus's Kingdom teaching. Even though the Kingdom comes as a man sowing good seed and is "now," there will be mixture until the harvest.

The arrival of the Kingdom does not necessarily mean the arrival of the judgment of the wicked. God will allow the wicked to grow in His kingdom until the end of the age. At the end of the age He will harvest the righteous and the unrighteous in resurrection and divide them in judgment.

Jesus explains this to His disciples later:

> this world

29

> *Then he left the crowds and went into the house. And his disciples came to him, saying, "Explain to us the parable of the weeds of the field." ³⁷He answered, "The one who sows the good seed is the Son of Man. ³⁸The field is the world, and the good seed is the sons of the kingdom. The weeds are the sons of the evil one, ³⁹and the enemy who sowed them is the devil. The harvest is the end of the age, and the reapers are angels. ⁴⁰Just as the weeds are gathered and burned with fire, so will it be at the end of the age. ⁴¹The Son of Man will send his angels, and they will gather out of his kingdom all causes of sin and all law-breakers, ⁴²and throw them into the fiery furnace. In that place there will be weeping and gnashing of teeth. ⁴³Then the righteous will shine like the sun in the kingdom of their Father. He who has ears, let him hear. (Matthew 13:36-43) ESV*

He taught that while the parable compared the one who sows the good seed to the Kingdom itself, the sower is "the son of Man." Christ is the sower, and His rule is the Kingdom. The field is this present world (this age). The harvest is the end of the age and the inauguration of the age to come. This age ends with the angels (the reapers) gathering the wicked and condemning them to punishment. The righteous will "shine like the sun in the kingdom of their Father." Even though the Kingdom was "now" in the sowing, it is "not yet" in its full realization.

This passage gives the same contrast between this age and the age to come as Luke 20:34-36:

This age	The resurrection and the age that follows
Mixture of good and bad	The righteous
Natural men	The righteous shine like the sun

What may be even more important in sorting out how complicated end times studies have become is that verses 40 and 41 clearly show that the present age ends with the coming of "The Son of Man." The second coming of Christ is when the gathering and sorting will occur. The Kingdom, the "not yet," and the age to come will arrive, and there will be no more mixture of righteous and unrighteous.

The Parable of the Mustard Seed

Jesus followed the parable of the weeds with the parable of the Mustard Seed. While this parable is broad and has many applications, Jesus gave this parable in the context of end time teaching, and it is appropriate to view it from that lens.

31He put another parable before them, saying, "The kingdom of heaven is like a grain of mustard seed that a man took and sowed in his field.32It is the smallest of all seeds, but when it has grown it is larger than all the garden plants and becomes a tree, so that the birds of the air come and make nests in its branches." (Matthew 13:31-32) ESV

The Kingdom of heaven arrives as a seed (this age) and grows and expands until its full consummation (the second coming and the age to come). In its full consummation it is a tree large enough for the birds to nest in it. This may be an allusion to Nebuchadnezzar's dream in Daniel 4 where Nebuchadnezzar dreams of a tree so large it covers the whole earth and the birds, who are the nations, rest in its branches. We can expect all the Kingdom to spread through the nations.

The Parable of the Leaven

The parable of the leaven is similar.

> *He told them another parable. "The kingdom of heaven is like leaven that a woman took and hid in three measures of flour, till it was all leavened."*
> *(Matthew 13:33) ESV*

Again, the Kingdom comes and arrives (this age, the "now") and then spreads/grows until it has changed the nature of everything (the age to come, "the not yet").

The Treasure and the Pearl

> *44 "The kingdom of heaven is like treasure hidden in a field, which a man found and covered up. Then in his joy he goes and sells all that he has and buys that field. (Matthew 13:44) ESV*

The Kingdom is present but hidden (this age, the "now"). Those who discover it are full of the joy of its worth and are willing to make the complete sacrifice the kingdom requires.

> *45 "Again, the kingdom of heaven is like a merchant in search of fine pearls, 46 who, on finding one pearl of great value, went and sold all that he had and bought it. (Matthew 13:45-46) ESV*

The kingdom is like a man searching for fine pearls (the "now"). Remember that Jesus also said that the Kingdom was the "Son of Man." When the Kingdom (or the Son of Man) finds the object of its search it gives all that it has to acquire its treasure. Jesus seeks to save that which was lost and gives His life and all that He has to acquire us.

The Parable of the Dragnet

Jesus completed this section of parables in Matthew by reemphasizing many of the points he made in the parable of the tares.

"Again, the kingdom of heaven is like a net that was thrown into the sea and gathered fish of every kind. ⁴⁸When it was full, men drew it ashore and sat down and sorted the good into containers but threw away the bad. ⁴⁹So it will be at the end of the age. The angels will come out and separate the evil from the righteous ⁵⁰and throw them into the fiery furnace. In that place there will be weeping and gnashing of teeth. (Matthew 13:47-50) ESV

The kingdom arrives first in a fishing phase (this age, the "now"). The fishing phase is characterized by mixture of both good and bad. The Kingdom then arrives in a gathering and sorting phase. This is the resurrection and the judgment (the age to come and the not yet). A mixture exists on the earth and *in the kingdom* until then. Jesus is clear that the judgment occurs "at the end of the age."

Jesus's parables were messages rich with meaning. They were simple and memorable. Each contained a simple message yet gave a wealth of information. Jesus's parables are concentrated with information about the end times, but they were hardly the only place Jesus addressed the issue. In the next chapter we will take a look at how Jesus developed his teaching about the two ages, sometimes in unlikely places.

No !.!

No
They are about the Kingdom

33

CHAPTER 6: JESUS AND THE TWO AGES

While the "Now and Not Yet" themes of the Kingdom are often beneath the surface throughout Jesus's teaching, the Two Ages scheme explicitly shows up again and again. The apostles heard about the Two Ages through Jesus's ministry and continued to pass on Jesus's teaching as a key to understanding the end times. In the next two chapters we will investigate the rest of what Jesus taught about the Two Ages, and combine it with what we've learned in Luke 20 and the end time Parables.

Blasphemy against the Holy Spirit

Casting out demons was a hallmark of Jesus's ministry, but not everyone was convinced that He had God-given authority over demons. Some of the religious leaders posited that the reason Jesus could cast out demons was because He was actually in league with them. Jesus's answer in Matthew 12 reveals much about deliverance ministry, the supernatural world, and the end times.

---

30 Whoever is not with me is against me, and whoever does not gather with me scatters. 31 Therefore I tell you, every sin and blasphemy will be forgiven people, but the blasphemy against the Spirit will not be forgiven. 32 And whoever speaks a word against the Son of Man will be forgiven, but whoever speaks against the Holy Spirit will not be forgiven, either in this age or in the age to come. (Matthew 12:30-32) ESV

When we compare this passage to its parallel in Mark 3:29 it reveals that "this age" and "the age to come," comprise all time. A sin that is not forgiven in either age is an "eternal sin" according to Mark 3:29. Therefore the two ages cover all of time, including eternity.

To some this may seem obvious, but it is an important point. "Blasphemy against the spirit" is not forgiven in "this age or in the age to come." It is an "eternal sin." "This age" and "the age to come" include all of time from Genesis until the return of Christ and all of eternity.

Leaving Everything

---

28 Peter began to say to him, "See, we have left everything and followed you." 29 Jesus said, "Truly, I say to you, there is no one who has left house or brothers or sisters or mother or father or children or lands, for my sake and for the gospel, 30 who will not receive a hundredfold now in this time, houses and brothers and sisters and mothers and children and lands, with persecutions, and in the age to come eternal life. 31 But many who are first will be last, and the last first." Mark 10:28-30 ESV
28 And Peter said, "See, we have left our homes and followed you." 29 And he said to them, "Truly, I say to you, there is no one who has left house or wife or brothers or parents or children, for the sake of the kingdom of God, 30 who will not receive many times more in this time, and in the age to come eternal life." (Luke 19:28-30) ESV

Jesus taught his disciples that persecution would be a part of their experience in "this age," but that they would receive eternal life "in the age to come." When you compare this passage with its parallel in Luke 19:30 we see that "this time" is a synonym for "this age." Jesus is referring to the state of the world in this current time frame when he refers to "this age."

These are simple and straightforward points taken directly from Scripture. Jesus used the Two Ages to teach about the end times and teach people that the future and the age to come would be different from "this age." We can add what we've learned here to the chart we made from Luke 20:

This Age	In the resurrection and the age that follows
Marriage	There is no marriage
Death	There is no death
Mixture of worthy and unworthy	Only the worthy sons of God exist
Natural men	Resurrected men
Seed time	Harvest
Fishing phase	Gathering and sorting
Kingdom in Seed form	Kingdom in full form
Persecution and Trouble	Eternal life and Reward

This list combines the two age passages with the parables. In the next chapter we will look at what the rest of the New Testament says about the two ages, form some simple conclusions, and see how this teaching fits with some of the different views on the end times.

CHAPTER 7: THE TWO AGES AND THE NEW TESTAMENT

The New Testament authors had many more things to say about the two ages throughout the epistles. I'm going to focus in on the verses that are most important for our study and reveal the most information about the end times. But first, I want to lay down some basic theology about this age and the age to come from a few foundational verses.

The Gospel and the Two Ages

---

4 who gave himself for our sins to deliver us from the present evil age, according to the will of our God and Father, (Galatians 1:4) ESV

This present age is evil. Jesus gave Himself for our sins in order to deliver us from this present evil age. He gave Himself for our sins, so we could be part of the age to come.

and we are part of the Age to Come Now !!

We know that we are of God, and the whole world lies under the sway of the wicked one. (1 John 5:19) ESV

The whole world is under the sway, power, and rule of the devil. When sin entered the world, each human being was born corrupted. Adam enslaved the world to sin: "Jesus answered them, 'Most assuredly, I say to you, whoever commits sin is a slave of sin'" (John 8:34 NKJV). The whole world lives as slaves of the sin, yet they were made to rule and made for love. They live addicted and enslaved, afraid and alone, bitter, wounded, "foolish, disobedient, deceived, serving various lusts and pleasures, living in malice and envy, hateful and hating one another" (Titus 3:3 NKJV): a tortured existence without God and without hope. "But when the kindness and love of God our savior toward man appeared..." (Titus 3:3 NKJV) He saved us.

This is the wonderful Good News, the appearance of the kindness and love of God our Savior. That's Jesus, God in human flesh who came not to destroy men's lives but to save them (Luke 9:56 NKJV). "The reason the Son of God appeared was to destroy the works of the devil" (1 John 3:8 ESV). Jesus appeared in kindness and love to destroy the yoke of slavery, to demolish the rule of the devil over man, to save us from sin and evil, and to give us abundant life in the love and favor of the Father.

Though the devil rules this world through sin, Jesus has come and defeated the power of sin and death. He has risen to obtain a name above every name that at the name of Jesus every knee will bow, and every tongue confess that Christ is Lord (Phil 2:10-11). All authority has been given to the Lord Jesus (Matt 28:18), and at the end of time, He will come as the King of Kings and Lord of Lords, giving justice to all who rejected His love and lordship. Now he waits, not willing

He himself said: I saw satan fall like lightening from heaven.

that any should perish under His justice, but giving all men time to turn and come under the rule of love.

He has commissioned us to spread that Kingdom, rule, and sovereignty over all the earth, declaring the Good News. The rule of Christ, the Kingdom of God, the sovereignty of Jesus, is Good News. It's a message of forgiveness and love, of life and blessing, of salvation from sin and destruction for all who call on the name of Jesus in faith. May Christ be manifest in us to destroy the work and rule of the devil as we spread God's kingdom and sovereignty over all the earth declaring the Gospel of salvation and urging all men to make Jesus their Lord. Satan rules over this world (1 John 5:19, Eph 2:2). God rules over us.

2 Corinthians 4:4

---

4 In their case the god of this world has blinded the minds of the unbelievers, to keep them from seeing the light of the gospel of the glory of Christ, who is the image of God. ESV

The god of this world is Satan. He rules this age on earth. Jesus rules in the age to come.

$\frac{1}{2}$

Romans 12:2

Ps. 2 The KING of KINGS is ruling [All things] the whole Cosmos now → all authority...

Do not be conformed to this world [this age], but be transformed by the renewal of your mind, that by testing you may discern what is the will of God, what is good and acceptable and perfect. ESV

We live in this present age, but Christ commands us to live in step with Him instead of in step with this world. We are to live according

The Holy Spirit [GOD] has invaded this dark evil age with His New Age (the Age to Come) has come into this age!

in eternity
=
↑

to the Kingdom of Christ and the age to come. In the age to come God's desire will be done perfectly. In the present age we must make an effort (2 Peter 1:5) to know and accomplish His will.

1 Corinthians 1:20

---

20 Where is the one who is wise? Where is the scribe? Where is the debater of this age? Has not God made foolish the wisdom of the world? ESV

The wisdom of this age is not the wisdom of the age to come.

1 Corinthians 2:6–8

---

6 Yet among the mature we do impart wisdom, although it is not a wisdom of this age or of the rulers of this age, who are doomed to pass away. 7 But we impart a secret and hidden wisdom of God, which God decreed before the ages for our glory. 8 None of the rulers of this age understood this, for if they had, they would not have crucified the Lord of glory. (ESV)

This age and the rulers of this age are temporary. The age to come is eternal. It was the rulers of this age who crucified Jesus. This age and its rulers are evil. The age to come is an age of God's perfect rule.

Ephesians 1:21

---

21 far above all rule and authority and power and dominion, and above every name that is named, not only in this age but also in the one to come. (ESV)

Eph. 1:1-20
Eph. 5:8-17
6+pose

living in a dark world
among children of darkness. Col. 1:12-14

Jesus's rule is now. He reigns and rules far above all rule and authority and power and dominion. He rules in this age and He rules in the age to come. His rule is in seed form now, but it is spreading its branches out. It is spreading through the world like leaven through dough, and it will cover the whole earth in the age to come.

1 Timothy 6:17–18

17 As for the rich in this present age, charge them not to be haughty, nor to set their hopes on the uncertainty of riches, but on God, who richly provides us with everything to enjoy. 18 They are to do good, to be rich in good works, to be generous and ready to share, (ESV)

Paul instructs Timothy to teach the rich in this age to store up treasures in the age to come. The riches of this age are different from the riches of the age to come.

Titus 2:12

12 training us to renounce ungodliness and worldly passions, and to live self-controlled, upright, and godly lives in the present age, (ESV)

This age is an age of training in righteousness. In the age to come, righteousness will be perfected.

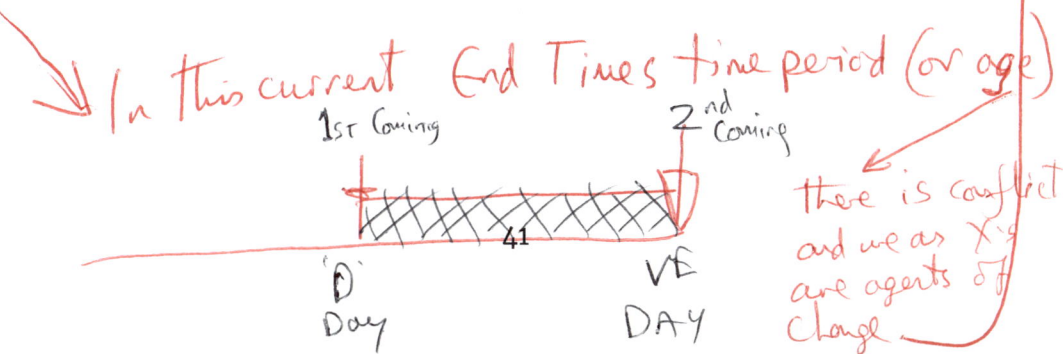

called, privileged to be children of light

In this current End Times time period (or age)

1st Coming   2nd Coming

41

'D'
Day

VE
DAY

there is conflict and we as X's are agents of change.

YES ✓ :)

Hebrews 6:5

---

5 and have tasted the goodness of the word of God and the powers of the age to come, (ESV)

The age to come is characterized by supernatural power which we taste and see in this age. Supernatural miracles and gifts are tastes of the age to come. When we enjoy God's glory in heaven, all things will be sustained in perfection by supernatural power and wisdom.

Conclusions

Yahweh reigns supreme over all of Creation, but Satan has gained authority over humanity and this age and its systems because of humanity's sin. Christ reigns in His Kingdom, and in the age to come His Kingdom will overcome all of humanity and every system of the world.

Those who submit to Christ and His Kingdom must learn to live contrary to this world and its systems. We must seek to accomplish God's will on this earth while we wait to see His will done perfectly in the age to come and in the new earth. This age, its wisdom, and its riches are temporary and can't be compared to the glory of to the age to come. We are pilgrims traveling through a world overrun with the enemy. The obstacles and adversity we encounter in this age help us grow in righteousness and anticipate the age to come. And as we walk in this age, we see Christ bring his miraculous strength and power into this age. The age to come will last forever.

These simple truths taught throughout the New Testament create a picture of this world and how it relates to the next. In the next chapter, we will see how these simple truths can help us understand the most complex end times controversies.

Better: The Holy Spirit has been sent by Jesus to overrun (= invade) this dark world with (His) LIGHT. See from the Day of Pentecost onwards

CHAPTER 8: WHAT THE TWO AGES TEACHING REVEALS ABOUT THE END

This age" Began at creation and the beginning of time. All of the Bible's teaching about "this age" present it as the normal, earthly order of life. When Jesus taught that "the sons of this age marry," in Luke 20:34 (ESV) he was teaching that marriage, a covenant instituted by God at the creation of human beings, is part of "this age." Only a supernatural transformation of the world will change our relationships so dramatically that marriage will no longer exist.

In the same way Paul's teaching about "the rich in this present age" (1 Tim 6:17 ESV) implies that "this age" spans the whole of history when some people have had more than others. The age to come is an age of a different kind of riches.

The Bible also teaches that this present age is evil, and that Satan is the god of this age. Was this only true during the time of the New

Testament? Clearly the world has been evil, and Satan has had his way in it, since sin first came into the world. "This age" is characterized by the natural order of the world created by God and then corrupted by the fall of man. "This age" began in Genesis 1-3.

The Two Ages Cover All of Time

Another important but simple point about the Two Ages is that they cover all of time. This age spans from the beginning of time until the arrival of the age to come. The age to come covers the eternal state (which goes on forever).

In Matthew 12:32 Jesus teaches that blasphemy against the Holy Spirit will not be forgiven in this age or the age to come. This implies that blasphemy against the Holy Spirit will never be forgiven, but Mark 3:29 clarifies this by stating that blasphemy against the Holy Spirit is an "eternal sin." It is never forgiven. This age and the age to come cover the entire span of time.

This is corroborated in Mark 10:29 -30 which state that eternal life is received in the age to come. Similarly, in 1 Tim 6:17-19 Paul teaches that eternal life and true riches are in the future rather than in "this present age." All of human history, time, and eternity are encompassed in the two ages: this age of natural order and the age to come of eternal life.

This Age is evil and The Age to Come is Perfect

We have covered this point pretty clearly in previous sections but let me conclude that "this age" is evil and natural according to Romans 12:2, 1 Corinthians 2:6-8, Galatians 1:4, 2 Corinthians 4:4. Conversely "the age to come" is depicted as perfected and righteous in Luke 20, 1 Tim 6:17-19, Hebrews 6:5, Mark 10:29-30. While Jesus and the New Testament refer to the Kingdom and the Gospel as growing and progressing, the "age to come" arrives more suddenly.

NO! The Age to Come HAS ARRIVED in Jesus' Resurrection, the Outpouring of the HS, and The current rule of Christ.

45

In Luke 20 the age to come arrives with the resurrection of the dead and the supernatural transformation of the world. In the parables it arrives with the angels gathering the harvest and preparing for the judgment. "This age" will not grow into "the age to come." The age to come will arrive with enormous changes.

This Age is Ending

Titus 2:12 characterizes "this age" as a time of training. 1 Corinthians 2:6-8 states that the rulers of this age are doomed to pass away. Galatians 1:4 puts our deliverance from this "present" evil age in view, and the whole of Scripture testifies that this age is ending that we are in the process of ushering in "the age to come" and the day of the Lord (1 John 2:17).

The Age to Come is Beginning and Breaks into this Age

Hebrews 6:4-6 clearly states that the powers of the age to come can be tasted and seen in "this age." This confirms the "now" and "not yet" presence of the Kingdom of God. Every healing that we see, every miracle, every demon cast out is the arrival of the Kingdom of God (Luke 11:20).

Jesus instructed us to pray that God's Kingdom would come, and that God's will would be done here on earth as it is in heaven. This is a request for the age to come to break into this age. This is a prayer for the powers of the age to come to break into this world. And God is answering these prayers. We pursue spreading the rule of Christ throughout the earth, contending with the powers of this age.

An age is coming when we will no longer have to contend against the powers of this world. In fact, the last enemy will be defeated, death. We will live in resurrected bodies and death will no longer come for any of us. Until that time, we are in a "present, evil age," but experiencing the rule of Christ and the powers of the age to come breaking into this age.

What Divides the Two Ages? The Judgment

The age to come and the Kingdom of God have broken into this age, but there is a clear dividing line between the two. This age has a definite end and the age to come has a definite beginning. The Bible states again and again that the end of this age and the beginning of the age to come occurs on a single day. This is known as the day of the Lord. The day of the Lord begins with the return of Christ who will judge the wicked and resurrect the righteous. This will end this age and inaugurate the age to come.

- Luke 20:35 states that "attaining to that age" is the same as "attaining resurrection of the dead." This age ends at the resurrection. The age to come begins at the resurrection of the dead.
- The resurrection occurs at Christ's return. (1 Cor 15:22-23, 50-55, 1 Thess 4:16)
- Matthew 13:39-43 refers to the same event as Luke 20:35 — the judgment of the wicked and the resurrection of the righteous which will occur at the second coming (Matt 24:30, 31, 25:31).
- In the age to come we receive eternal life (Mark 10:30). This occurs at Christ's second coming (Matt 25:31, 46).
- Titus 2:11-13 and Matt 28:20 teaches that the second coming ends this age and brings the fullness of the age to come. Jesus promises to be with us to the end of this age because we know that He will be with us in full perception in the age to come.

The day of the Lord when Christ returns will be the last day of "this age" and the first day of "the age to come." If this is true, where can we place Christ's reign on the earth? What about the passages that have been interpreted as Christ's kingdom before the resurrection? These questions have been raised since the beginning of church history. We will apply what we've discussed so far to answer these questions in the next chapter.

CHAPTER 9: THE TWO AGES AND THE THIRD AGE

he two ages may seem simple, but this simple teaching has profound effects on our view of the end times. These simple truths, most of which I held long before I had my end time views figured out, actually give us the tools to answer many of the most difficult end times questions. Of the three main views of eschatology—premillennialism, postmillennialism, and amillennialism—only two views fit with the two-age scheme.

Amillennialism asserts that Christ's earthly reign is now through the church and that reign will become physical only in the New Heavens and the New Earth. Christ reigns through the church now and spreads His rule through His church. Christ will come back. The dead will be raised. The wicked will be judged. The righteous will enter the eternal state. There will be a new heaven and a new earth. This is consistent with what we have learned about the Two Ages.

Postmillennialism asserts that Christ's earthly reign is either now or in the future of "this age." Christ reigns through the church now and the church's success will usher in Christ's physical reign when the majority of the world becomes believers and submit to Him. After this Millennial Age Christ will come back. The dead will be raised. The wicked will be judged. The righteous will enter the eternal state. There will be a new heaven and a new earth. While I disagree with postmillennialism for other reasons, this too can be consistent with the two ages.

Premillennialism asserts that Christ's earthly reign will occur in the future after his return but before the resurrection of the wicked and the judgment. In this view the world will get worse. Christ will come back. The Christian dead will be raised. Christ will reign on the earth physically for one thousand years. Satan will be loosed. There will be an apostasy and rebellion of the nations. Christ will destroy the wicked. The wicked will be resurrected to judgment. The righteous will be rewarded and enter the eternal state. There will be a new heaven and a new earth.

This is not consistent with the two ages. Where in the two ages does Christ's physical reign fit if it is after "this age" but before "the age to come?" Christ's reign becomes a kind of "third age" that doesn't have the characteristics of "this age" or the characteristics of the "age to come." It doesn't fit the scheme.

Premillennialism asserts that physical death will continue beyond Christ's second coming. During Christ's thousand-year reign people are still mortal and still die. There are several problems with this view beyond the two ages. We know that death will be defeated when Christ returns and the resurrection occurs (1 Cor 15). Yet according to premillennialism, believers and unbelievers will still die after the end of this age.

Premillennialism also asserts that natural creation will continue after Christ's second coming, and that natural creation will be subject to the Fall and the curse of sin. This doesn't fit the two-age scheme either. Christ returns, but sin prevails as does the mixture of the righteous and the wicked? People still rebel against Christ? That would mean that Christ returns, but human beings will still live in "this age" rather than in the "age to come."

Premillennialism's fundamental assertion is that there is a physical millennium of Christ's rule after Christ returns but before the eternal state. This means that evil un-resurrected men live alongside righteous resurrected men after the return of Christ. This cannot fit the two ages because the millennium won't fit into either age. It can't fit into "this age" because "this age" ends with Christ's return. It can't fit into "the age to come" because "the age to come" does not contain mixture. It only contains righteous resurrected men. No unrighteous un-resurrected men are in "the age to come." Premillennialism essentially asserts that there is a third age between the two ages that doesn't fit Christ's description of "this age" or Christ's description of "the age to come." If the two ages as Christ and the apostles taught it is (and as we understand it) accurate, then premillennialism is false.

Dr. Sam Storms identifies these six problems with premillennialism:

---

1.   *You must necessarily believe that physical death will continue to exist beyond the time of Christ's second coming.*
2.   *You must necessarily believe that the natural creation will continue, beyond the time of Christ's second coming, to be subjected to the curse imposed by the fall of man.*
3.   *You must necessarily believe that the New Heavens and New Earth will not be introduced until 1,000 years subsequent to the return of Christ.*
4.   *You must necessarily believe that unbelieving men and women will still have the opportunity to come to saving faith in Christ for at least 1,000 years subsequent to his return.*
5.   *You must necessarily believe that unbelievers will not be finally resurrected until at least 1,000 years subsequent to the return of Christ.*

6. You must necessarily believe that unbelievers will not be finally judged and cast into eternal punishment until at least 1,000 years subsequent to the return of Christ.[5]

But can the truth about the end times really be as simple as the two ages suggest? Is there anywhere where the Bible lays out the whole timeline this way? In the next chapter, we will look at the Bible's clearest and most systematic teaching about the end times.

---

[5] Storms, S. (2009, October 7). Problems with premillennialism [Blog post]. Retrieved from https://www.thegospelcoalition.org/blogs/justin-taylor/what-you-must-believe-if-you-are-a-premillennialist/

CHAPTER 10: PETER'S TEACHING

So, I hear you have been doing quite a study on [end time] Bible prophecy," my friend John said.

"Yes," I said.

"So, what's your view on all this that's happening?"

"My end times view is 2 Peter Chapter 3," I said.

When people ask me what my view of the end times is, I often say, "2 Peter Chapter 3." In discussions about the end times I often ask, "What does 2 Peter Chapter 3 say?" I believe that this passage is the clearest systematic teaching on the end times that we have in Scripture. The context of the passage is Peter's correction of false teaching about the end times, and he takes the opportunity to lay out the major events in clear and simple language.

While the book of Revelation contains many more details and covers the end times in greater breadth, few would argue that it is clearer or more general than 2 Peter 3. If this is true about 2 Peter 3, shouldn't we take 2 Peter 3 at face value and interpret the book of Revelation (a symbolic visionary experience) to be consistent with it? I would argue that we should. But most Bible prophecy teachers don't treat 2 Peter 3 this way. Instead they reinterpret what Peter wrote to fit their interpretation of Revelation.

This is now the second letter that I am writing to you, beloved. In both of them I am stirring up your sincere mind by way of reminder, 2 that you should remember the predictions of the holy prophets and the commandment of the Lord and Savior through your apostles, 3 knowing this first of all, that scoffers will come in the last days with scoffing, following their own sinful desires. 4 They will say, "Where is the promise of his coming? For ever since the fathers fell asleep, all things are continuing as they were from the beginning of creation." (2 Peter 3:1-4) ESV

Peter opens this section of his epistle with a warning to his listeners that scoffers or mockers will come. These scoffers do not believe that Jesus will return. They argue that it has been too long, and that Jesus is not returning at all. The atheists among today's intellectuals could easily fit this profile. They mock the fact that we are still waiting for the return of Christ 2000 years after He ascended. They point to the apostle's statements that Christ is returning soon and feel vindicated in their unbelief. Similarly, postmodern Bible scholars argue that this is one of the nonfactual parts of the Biblical myth. Full preterists or hyper-preterists also don't look towards a second coming. They assert that while Christ had not yet returned at the time of Peter's writing, He has already spiritually returned in 70AD and that we should no longer wait for the return of Christ.

God knew that all of these doubts and doubters would arise and used Peter to issue a timeless warning to all of us who live before the physical bodily return of Jesus Christ.

5 For they deliberately overlook this fact, that the heavens existed long ago, and the earth was formed out of water and through water by the word of God, 6 and that by means of these the world that then existed was deluged with water and perished. 7 But by the same word the heavens and earth that now exist are stored up for fire, being kept until the day of judgment and destruction of the ungodly. (2 Peter 3:5-7) ESV

Peter teaches that this current physical earth will be destroyed in the same way that the earth before the flood would be destroyed. He refers to the physical earth and to the flood of Genesis 6-8. God promised to never destroy the world by water again. But God will destroy this current earth through fire.

Another point that's vital to our study is that this earth is being kept "until" the day of judgment and destruction of the ungodly. The earth will remain unchanged until the day of judgment which will also be the day of the destruction of the godly. The judgment, the destruction of the wicked, and the destruction of the earth will occur on the same day.

8 But do not overlook this one fact, beloved, that with the Lord one day is as a thousand years, and a thousand years as one day. 9 The Lord is not slow to fulfill his promise as some count slowness, but is patient toward you, not wishing that any should perish, but that all should reach repentance. 10 But the day of the Lord will come like a thief, and then the heavens will pass away with a roar, and the heavenly bodies will be burned up and dissolved, and the earth and the works that are done on it will be exposed. (2 Peter 3:8-10) ESV

Peter continues his theme of disproving the mockers, reminding his readers that God is not slow to fulfill His promise, but that he is patient. Christ has not returned, and the day of the Lord has not come because God is giving human beings more time to repent. He desires more people to come into His kingdom.

Even though God is patient, the end will come suddenly and quickly. It will be unforeseen and, for many, unprepared for. Peter is clear that the heavens and the stars and the earth will be destroyed on "the day of the Lord." This adds to the point that the judgment, the destruction of the wicked, and the destruction of the earth will occur on the same day and that is the "day of the Lord" and the day of the Lord's return.

If this reading of Peter is accurate it does not fit with a physical millennial reign in the future. How can there be a millennial age on the earth after which the wicked on the earth rebel from Christ's rule if the wicked are judged and destroyed at Christ's return? How can there be a millennial rule on this earth before the end at all if the earth will be destroyed when Christ returns? Premillennialism asserts that Christ will return and set up His rule on the earth for 1000 years and only after all of that time will the wicked be judged and destroyed with the earth. But if we are reading Peter correctly, Christ's return, the judgment, and the destruction of the wicked will all occur on the same day in rapid succession.

---

11 Since all these things are thus to be dissolved, what sort of people ought you to be in lives of holiness and godliness, 12 waiting for and hastening the coming of the day of God, because of which the heavens will be set on fire and dissolved, and the heavenly bodies will melt as they burn! 13 But according to his promise we are waiting for new heavens and a new earth in which righteousness dwells. (2 Peter 3:11-13) ESV

Peter moves to application. He argues that the coming destruction of the earth should dramatically change how we live. We should focus

on the eternal, what will last. We should live holy, godly lives in view of the coming destruction. We should live in reverence and fear waiting for the new heavens and new earth. We look forward to the sudden supernatural transformation of the world where temporal things will be lost. Our houses will be gone along with our cars, our computers, and phones, our movies, and this book. Only people and God's Word will remain.

Is your understanding of the end times, the millennial reign, the rapture, or specific judgments consistent with what Peter writes here?

Do you believe that this earth will be destroyed, and that God will make a New Heavens and a New Earth? You might be surprised to learn that this doctrine is under attack. We will discuss why in the next chapter.

CHAPTER 11: THE NEW HEAVENS AND NEW EARTH

The Bible teaches that this earth will be destroyed, and that God will bring about a new heavens and a new earth. We look forward to this when Christ returns. Nevertheless, A popular teaching of partial preterists and full preterists is that the new heavens new earth are already here and that the old earth already passed away when the temple was destroyed in 70 AD. This chapter will depart from the larger picture and take a more concentrated look at one aspect of end times teaching—the New Heavens and New Earth.

Full and partial preterists cite some historic sources as evidence for their claim that there is no future or physical New Heavens and New Earth. One popular Bible teacher says

Clearly to take New Heavens and New Earth in a literal wooden fashion is akin to believing in childish fantasies such as Santa Claus and the Tooth fairy. Jesus and the Apostles of the first century were simply using the cultural vernacular of the day when they referred to the Old Covenant

Temple system being destroyed by fire as the "heavens and the earth passing away" and the New Covenant System taking its place as the "New Heavens and the New Earth."[6]

Preterists cite various passages in the Old and New Testament where they point to the words "heaven" and "earth" being used symbolically. They argue that "heaven" and "earth" are being used symbolically in 2nd Peter chapter 3 and Revelation 21 when the new heavens and new earth are discussed. They also cite a passage in Josephus's writings where he compares the Jewish temple's design to God's design of heaven and earth. Josephus was a first century Jewish historian whose life and work coincided with the lives of the apostles. While Josephus was not a believer, his work is one of the most important works we have for understanding the first century world.

I encourage you to read what Josephus said about the temple's design in the footnote below.[7]

---

[6] Welton, J. (2014, April 19). Literal new heavens and new earth? [Blog post]. Retrieved from (https://weltonacademy.com/blogs/jonathanwelton/50140161-literal-new-heaven-and-new-earth)

[7] ...for if any one do but consider the fabric of the tabernacle, and take a view of the garments of the high priest, and of those vessels which we make use of in our sacred ministration, he will find that our legislator was a divine man, and that we are unjustly reproached by others; for if any one do without prejudice, and with judgment, look upon these things, he will find they were everyone made in way of imitation and representation of the universe. When Moses distinguished the tabernacle into three parts, and allowed two of them to the priests, as a place accessible and common, he denoted the land and the seas, these being of general access to all; but he set apart the third division for God, because heaven is inaccessible to men. And when he ordered twelve loaves to be set on the table, he denoted the year, as distinguished into so many months. By branching out the candlestick into seventy parts, he secretly intimated the Decani, or seventy divisions of the planets; and as to the seven lamps upon the candlesticks, they referred to the course of the planets, of which that is the number. The veils, too, which were composed of four things, they declared the four elements; for the fine linen was proper to signify the earth, because the flax grows out of the earth; the purple signified the seas, because that color is dyed by the blood of a seas shell-fish; the blue is fit to signify the air; and the scarlet will naturally be an indication of fire. Now the vestment of the high priest being made of linen, signified the earth; the blue denoted the sky, being like lightning in its pomegranates, and in the noise of the bells resembling thunder. And for the ephod, it showed that God had made the universe of four elements; and as for the gold interwoven, I suppose it related to the splendor by which all things are enlightened. He also appointed the breastplate to be placed in the middle of the ephod, to resemble the earth, for that has the very middle place of the world. And the girdle which

Full and some partial preterists interpret what Josephus wrote here to argue that we are already living in the New Heavens and New Earth, and we don't look forward to the physical reality of the New Heaven and New Earth in the future. Josephus compared the temple design to God's design of heaven earth, but that does not mean that the ceiling of the Jewish temple was the seen as heaven and the floor of the temple was earth or that this was "cultural vernacular of the day." There is nothing in this quote that suggests this was cultural vernacular. If anything, Josephus's writing suggests the opposite. He suggests that some of what he wrote were his own thoughts rather than those of the culture.

In 1 Peter 3:1-4 Peter states that he is writing to specifically address those who do not believe that Christ is going to return. In our modern day, this is the full preterist view that Christ will not physically return. Peter is presenting an argument against scoffers and mockers in 2 Peter 3:5-7.

---

but they deliberately forget that long ago by God's Word the heavens came into being and the earth was formed out of water and by water by these waters also the world at that time was deluged and destroyed by the same word the present heavens and earth are reserved for fire being kept for the day of judgment and destruction of the ungodly (ESV)

Peter is clearly writing about the physical earth. The earth that was created by God's word and formed out of "water." He can't be talking about the temple here.

---

encompassed the high priest round, signified the ocean, for that goes round about and includes the universe. Each of the sardonyxes declares to us the sun and moon; those, I mean, that were in the nature of buttons on the high priest's shoulders. And for the twelve stones, whether we understand by them the months, or whether we understand the like number of the signs of that circle which the Greeks call the Zodiac, we shall not be mistaken in their meaning. And for the mitre, which was of a blue color, it seems to me to mean heaven; for how otherwise could the name of God be inscribed upon it? – Josephus

Peter states that this present heavens and earth, which he just clarified was physical, was being "reserved for fire." Peter clearly believed in a literal flood, and in God's literal promised not to destroy the earth with water after the flood. In the future God will destroy the earth by fire.

This is very clearly a physical earth that Peter is talking about, and it doesn't make any sense in context to switch to a symbolic or a spiritual heavens and earth.

In verses 8 through 10 Peter assured his readers that Christ was going to return and that when Christ returns the heavens will disappear with "a roar." That's an audible sound. Again, Peter gives physical descriptions.

This passage states that the elements are going to be destroyed by fire and part of the way preterists get around this is by saying that the word for "elements" is mistranslated, and that the word for "elements" can mean multiple different things. They argue that Peter is describing that the *order* of the earth will be destroyed, and "elements" refers to the system of law and the Jewish temple being destroyed. I do not think that makes any sense in the context of the passage and what Peter has been building in his argument. The only way to bring a discussion of the law and the Old Covenant system into the passage is by insisting on bringing it in because of a theological system like preterism.

Peter goes on in verses 11 through 13 to explain that this coming destruction of the earth is meant to change our lives. The preterist has to argue that this has already occurred and that it's not going to change our lives. Preterists must argue that Peter didn't write this to us but only to the believers of his day.

For those of us who believe this is still to come, Peter's words do change our lives. We understand this earth and things and it will not last. It's going to be destroyed, and we look forward to righteousness coming in a new heavens and a new earth. We look to invest in eternal things.

Peter states the elements are going to melt, and he says that the new heavens and the new earth will be a place where righteousness dwells, this will fulfill the longing of the Christian heart that longs for God to set all things right.

The New Heavens and New Earth in Revelation

Then I saw a new heaven and a new earth, for the first heaven and the first earth had passed away, and the sea was no more. 2 And I saw the holy city, new Jerusalem, coming down out of heaven from God, prepared as a bride adorned for her husband. 3 And I heard a loud voice from the throne saying, "Behold, the dwelling place of God is with man. He will dwell with them, and they will be his people, and God himself will be with them as their God. 4 He will wipe away every tear from their eyes, and death shall be no more, neither shall there be mourning, nor crying, nor pain anymore, for the former things have passed away." (Revelation 2:11-14) ESV

Revelation 2:11-14 is the second passage that clearly uses the term "new heavens in the new earth" (though the subject is referred to often in Scripture). Here John describes the new heavens and the new earth in symbolic language. While I agree with preterists that John's vision contains symbolism, I believe that what the symbolic language describes is a future event that will transform the world in a foundational way.

This passage promises that God will dwell with us. I see this truth as a "now and not yet" truth. God dwells with us in Christ, but He will dwell with us fully in the eternal state. It is possible to interpret this as a present reality. But verse four precludes an interpretation that rules out the future because it states that "death shall be no more." Clearly the New Jerusalem comes downs after the resurrection of the dead. First Corinthians 15 clearly states the last enemy to be defeated is death. The New Jerusalem will descend after the coming of Christ and after death is defeated. Our lives in the New Heavens and New Earth are part of the eternal state in the resurrection.

John also describes no more mourning or crying or pain. Clearly, we experience these things even though we have experienced new birth in Christ. This passage describes the world after its supernatural transformation. Preterism's argument that we already live in the symbolic New Heavens and New Earth cannot be supported by Scripture.

Why does this matter? Because God will fulfill many of his promises to his people in the new heaven and the new earth. Things on this earth will finally be set right. This is also important because preterists use this point to interpret Matthew 5:18 and Luke 16:17. This point impacts the rest of the preterist system of theology. Preterists argue that the Heavens and Earth have passed away and that the law has been made void as well. I believe the law endures, but we live in Christ who lives forever as our priest and sacrifice. He will continue to fulfill God's law for us until the end.

This book isn't the place to dive further into refuting preterism, but I hope that I have demonstrated that you can believe in Scripture's promise that God will bring about a New Heaven and a New Earth. This has been a departure away from the larger points about the end times, but our deeper dive into Peter's teaching about the New Heavens and New Earth will help us understand what Paul wrote about the end times in the next chapter.

CHAPTER 12: ~~PAUL'S~~ RESURRECTION TEACHING *through Paul*

Gods

Paul's writing about the Kingdom has a lot to tell us about the end times, but 1 Corinthians 15 may be his greatest revelation on the subject. In this chapter he not only proclaims the foundations of the gospel, but core truth about the resurrection of the dead, the age to come, and the return of Christ.

---

20 But in fact Christ has been raised from the dead, the firstfruits of those who have fallen asleep. 21 For as by a man came death, by a man has come also the resurrection of the dead. 22 For as in Adam all die, so also in Christ shall all be made alive. 23 But each in his own order: Christ the firstfruits, then at his coming those who belong to Christ. 24 Then comes the end, when he delivers the kingdom to God the Father after destroying every rule and every authority and power. 25 For he must reign until he has put all his enemies under his feet. 26 The last enemy to be destroyed is death. 27 For "God has put all things in subjection under his feet." But when it says, "all things are put in subjection," it is plain that he is excepted who put all things in subjection under him. 28 When all things are subjected to him, then the

Son himself will also be subjected to him who put all things in subjection under him, that God may be all in all. (1 Corinthians 15:20-28) ESV

Christ rose from the dead, and He is the first of the sons of God to do so. In the same way that Christ physically rose from the dead, those who have died in faith will also physically rise from the dead. While full preterists deny this truth and argue that the resurrection has already happened, the plain sense of Paul's teaching is that, like Christ, those who have died before the return of Christ will be rise from the dead.

In fact, in the same way that the entire human race inherited death from Adam, Christ will raise all from the dead. Every human being can look forward to the resurrection. The wicked will be raised into judgment, the righteous to everlasting life.

Paul even puts these events in order. Christ rose from the dead first. When He returns believers will rise from the dead. After this, the end of "this age" and this world as we know it will occur. Christ will deliver the kingdom of God to His Father having destroyed this world, its ruler, and all of His enemies (1 Corinthians 15:24). He will subject all earthly and spiritual rulers to His authority finally and fully.

Christ is reigning now. We will return to this, but Christ is reigning right now in His Kingdom. Before He has returned. Before the resurrection.

The resurrection is the final perfection of His rule. He is currently expanding His rule and reign through His Church, but when the end comes His kingdom will be fulfilled, perfected, and delivered to the Father into the eternal state. The conquest or conquering part of Christ's reign will end at the resurrection.

There will be no more rebellion. The church's mission on the earth of spreading His Kingdom throughout the world will be finished.

Christ Himself will take authority and every rebellious knee will bow. After the subjection of the earth and all the enemies of the spiritual realm, the last enemy will be defeated. That enemy is death.

Paul makes this clear in 1 Corinthians 15:50-55

---

50 I tell you this, brothers: flesh and blood cannot inherit the kingdom of God, nor does the perishable inherit the imperishable. 51 Behold! I tell you a mystery. We shall not all sleep, but we shall all be changed, 52 in a moment, in the twinkling of an eye, at the last trumpet. For the trumpet will sound, and the dead will be raised imperishable, and we shall be changed. 53 For this perishable body must put on the imperishable, and this mortal body must put on immortality. 54 When the perishable puts on the imperishable, and the mortal puts on immortality, then shall come to pass the saying that is written:

"Death is swallowed up in victory."

55 "O death, where is your victory?
O death, where is your sting?" (ESV)

The resurrection is the victory that swallows up death and the transformation that occurs in the resurrection can't help but remind us of Luke 20 when the supernatural transformation makes us sons of righteousness in the age to come without death or sin or marriage. We will have new bodies and new ways of relating to one another as we shine with the glory of God.

Death is defeated at the resurrection. Death is undone, and the righteous will enter the eternal state. After the resurrection no more enemies remain to be defeated. No earthly enemies can rebel. Death is the last enemy. No spiritual enemies can wage war against Christ or the Church. Death is the last enemy. No final apocalyptic battle awaits in the future. Death is the last enemy.

66

The resurrection marks the end of "this age" and all war and fighting. There can be no tribulation after the resurrection and the return of Christ. There can be no battle of Armageddon after the resurrection and the return of Christ. There can be no spiritual war after the resurrection and the return of Christ. If death is truly the last enemy to be defeated, then the resurrection marks the end of all war. The resurrection must occur after all tribulation and all battle both spiritual and earthly. Only after the defeat of every other enemy: sin, the world system with its kingdoms, the flesh, the principalities, Satan, and the wicked will death be defeated by the resurrection of the dead.

What does this have to do with the millennial reign? Premillennialists believe that Christ is going to return, raise believers from the dead and then reign for one thousand years on the earth. They believe that after these one thousand years, Satan will be released to wage war on the church; the nations of the earth will rebel against Christ leading to a final confrontation with all the armies of the earth. But all of this is supposed to occur after the resurrection according to the premillennial system.

Paul clearly teaches that death is the last enemy defeated at the resurrection, which means the tribulation and the final rebellion cannot occur after the resurrection. Paul teaches that Christ turns the kingdom and His reign over to the Father at this time. Christ won't begin His reign on the earth at His return and resurrection—He will conclude His earthly reign. Christ's return is the subject of the next chapter.

CHAPTER 13: PAUL'S TEACHING ON CHRIST'S RETURN

Paul not only wrote to the Corinthians extensively about the resurrection, he addressed the Thessalonians questions about the second coming of Christ. The Thessalonians had been taught that Jesus was coming back, and they believed it. They were looking forward to the imminent return of Christ. In fact, they were so convinced that it worried them that some people had died and missed Christ's return. They didn't have the advantage of being able to read the first letter to the Corinthians in their Bibles, so Paul had to write to them and address their concerns.

More than any other passage, 1 Thessalonians 4:13-18 has been used to justify the belief in a divine "rapture" of the church before the coming of Christ. The "rapture," or the belief that Jesus will return and remove Christians from the earth before the tribulation and before His final return, is the most identifiable part of dispensational Premillennialism and what *Left Behind* is all about.

There have been a number of books confronting the issue of the rapture and challenging it on a Biblical and historical basis. I will address the idea of the rapture here briefly while we look at the plain sense of what Paul wrote in his first letter to the Thessalonians, but the purpose of this book is less about dismantling the rapture and more about a different way of seeing the whole Bible's teaching about the end times.

Before jumping into what 1 Thessalonians does say about the return of Christ, I would like to make a point about what 1 Thessalonians and what the Bible does not say. Nowhere does the Bible say that there would be multiple returns of Christ. I would argue that a simple reading of the Scriptures does not mention the rapture anywhere. This is an argument from absence, and I know a difficult one to make, but my own convictions about the lack of a pretribulation rapture of the church were founded when I read the Bible multiple times and didn't find it anywhere.

John Macarthur, a famous apologist for dispensational premillennialism, has infamously written and taught that the doctrine of the rapture could be found in the white spaces between chapters 3 and 4 of the book Revelation.[8] Clearly, the absence of the rapture in the book of Revelation is a problem for dispensational premillennialists.

In approaching Paul's writing to the Thessalonians, we must remember that verse and chapter breaks were not an original part of the letter. We need to keep all of Paul's thoughts about the return of Christ together. I think 1 Thessalonians 5:1-11 is part of the same answer and same subject as 1 Thessalonians 4:13-18. I encourage you to go ahead and read the passage on your own and include some verses on either side of the passage for context.

---

[8] Macarthur, J. (2011). Truth endures: landmark sermons from forty years of unleashing God's truth. Wheaton, IL. Crossway. P.74

> 13 But we do not want you to be uninformed, brothers, about those who are asleep, that you may not grieve as others do who have no hope. 14 For since we believe that Jesus died and rose again, even so, through Jesus, God will bring with him those who have fallen asleep. (ESV)

Paul wrote to the Thessalonians to address a specific concern about those who had died before Christ returned. He assured the Thessalonians that they did not have to worry that those who had died before the return of Christ would miss anything.

We don't mourn as though those people are gone forever. We don't mourn as though those people will miss out on the return of Christ. God will raise them from the dead in the same way that He rose Christ from the dead (v. 14). In fact, they will rise and come with Christ.

> 15 For this we declare to you by a word from the Lord, that we who are alive, who are left until the coming of the Lord, will not precede those who have fallen asleep. 16 For the Lord himself will descend from heaven with a cry of command, with the voice of an archangel, and with the sound of the trumpet of God. And the dead in Christ will rise first. (1 Thessalonians 4:15-16) ESV

Paul begins to prophesy here and speak from apostolic revelation. Those who have died before the return of Christ will enjoy and witness His return before we do. Christ will descend from heaven and the dead in Christ will rise from the graves and rise from the earth to meet Christ. But notice how Christ returns. Does He return secretly? Does He return invisibly? Is this a secret or silent rapture where everyone disappears?

Yes

Contrary to the teaching about the rapture, Christ comes with a loud cry, the shout of angels, and the trumpet of God. This will be loud, and the whole world will know. This goes completely against the idea that Christ is returning secretly to rapture the church. Christ is returning to conquer and receive the earth.

---

17 Then we who are alive, who are left, will be caught up together with them in the clouds to meet the Lord in the air, and so we will always be with the Lord. 18 Therefore encourage one another with these words. (1 Thessalonians 4:17-18) ESV

Those who are on the earth will rise to meet the resurrected saints and Christ in the air, taking part in the public display of Christ's glory and the defeat of His enemies. This is the end of the earth. We aren't deserting the earth here; we the church are part of ending the earth as we know it and bringing about the new Heavens and the New Earth.

Now concerning the times and the seasons, brothers, you have no need to have anything written to you. 2 For you yourselves are fully aware that the day of the Lord will come like a thief in the night. 3 While people are saying, "There is peace and security," then sudden destruction will come upon them as labor pains come upon a pregnant woman, and they will not escape. (1 Thessalonians 5:1-3) ESV

Paul goes on to write more about the return of Christ. He isn't changing the subject here but continuing on his theme. He lets the Thessalonians know that no one will be able to predict Christ's return. It will be a sudden surprise. It will come when the wicked do not expect it. And this too is a problem for those who argue that 1 Thessalonians is about a rapture of the church. Because here it says that "sudden destruction" will come upon the wicked at the return of Christ. Christ is not returning for His church at one stage, and then waiting to destroy the wicked a millennium later. Christ's return resurrects the dead, gathers the church, and destroys the wicked. There is only one day of the Lord and only one return of Christ.

---

4 But you are not in darkness, brothers, for that day to surprise you like a thief. 5 For you are all children of light, children of the day. We are not of the night or of the darkness. 6 So then let us not sleep, as others do, but let us keep awake and be sober. 7 For those who sleep, sleep at night, and those who get drunk, are drunk at night. 8 But since we belong to the day, let us be sober, having put on the breastplate of faith and love, and for a helmet the hope of salvation. 9 For God has not destined us for wrath, but to obtain salvation through our Lord Jesus Christ, 10 who died for us so that whether we are awake or asleep we might live with him. 11 Therefore encourage one another and build one another up, just as you are doing. (1 Thessalonians 5:4-11) ESV

Paul moves on to application and tells the Thessalonians how to apply this information. He does not caution them that failing to be ready for the return of Christ will result in being left behind, instead he encourages them to stay awake in order to avoid "wrath"—the final destruction of the Kingdom of Darkness. He assures them of his confidence in them that they are awake. They are behaving as those who are aware of the Kingdom and the King's return. They are not people who believe that the master is away or that their evil deeds will not be seen. They have maintained faith and righteousness, and because of that they can look forward to salvation and living with Christ forever. They will be part of the return of Christ, the resurrection of the dead, the defeat of Christ's enemies, and the eternal state in the age to come. They will be honored at the judgment seat of Christ, the subject of the next chapter.

CHAPTER 14: THE FINAL JUDGMENT

Ernie was drunk. It was a hot day, and he was soaked with sweat. He cried for most of the Bible study. He slurred his words through tears and drunkenness. He told me how much he loved me and how ashamed he was.

When the Bible study was over, and I was preparing to leave, he was still sobbing. He told me he loved me again and came towards me for a hug. This huge drunk man covered in hot slime and reeking of alcohol, body odor, and poverty moved towards me with his arms out. Time froze for a second. In that split moment of time I heard a whisper, "What you do for the least of these, you do unto Me."

Suddenly Ernie was Jesus. I wrapped my arms around him. He sobbed into my shoulder. His sweat soaked my shirt. He smelled like love. This was what it was all about.

Months later the police found Ernie's body in an alley.

I believe that "the judge of all the earth will do right" (Genesis 18:25). I hope that when I stand before Jesus, I have done something for the least of these.

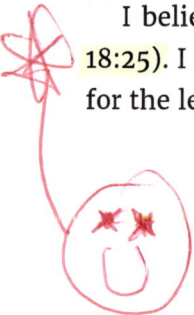

The Judgment Seat

Before we move on and look at the book of Revelation and the passages about the reign of Christ, we will look at the final judgment and what examining those passages in their context reveals.

So whether we are at home or away, we make it our aim to please him. 10 For we must all appear before the judgment seat of Christ, so that each one may receive what is due for what he has done in the body, whether good or evil. (2 Corinthians 5:9-10) ESV

God

In 2 Corinthians Paul writes that all of us will appear at the judgment seat of Christ. These verses come right after a discussion of the resurrection of the body. Paul teaches that the judgment seat of Christ will occur after the resurrection of the dead. Paul also writes that we will receive what is due to us according to our deeds "whether good or evil." This suggests that those who undergo this judgment will receive both rewards and punishment. Jesus is not only giving out rewards at this judgment; he is also judging people for their evil deeds.

Some premillennialists argue that because the Greek word for "seat" in this passage is different than the word used in other passages describing judgment, that this passage relates to a judgment for believers only, and that this is a judgment where Christ will give rewards to believers. They refer to this as the *bema* seat and contrast it with the "White Throne" judgment in Revelation 20:11-15.

There are several reasons why I do not see this in the text. The primary reason is that the passage mentions both good and evil. You must either claim that believers will receive punishments as well as

75

rewards or that both believers and unbelievers will be judged at the same time.

Another reason is that I don't find the argument over the wording for "seat" convincing. The fact that Paul chose a different word for "seat" than the word John uses for "throne" does not mean that they are talking about different events. It's even more of a stretch to base an entire doctrine about separate judgments on such a small variation in word choice, when the rest of the content remains consistent.

We make every effort to please God while we live on earth in this body because we look forward to standing before the judgment seat of Christ. We will be judged according to our deeds, and both good and evil deeds will be judged at that time.

The Sheep and the Goats

What Paul writes is consistent with the messages that Jesus gave about the judgment. Matthew 25:31-46 features the lengthiest passage about the judgment and is in the context of several parables and teachings about the end times. Some premillennial scholars argue that this passage is a parable, but the text itself does not say that. Jesus told two parables in Matthew 25 using words to signify a parable ("will be like"). He began this teaching without comparative words.

---

31 "When the Son of Man comes in his glory, and all the angels with him, then he will sit on his glorious throne. 32 Before him will be gathered all the nations, and he will separate people one from another as a shepherd separates the sheep from the goats. 33 And he will place the sheep on his right, but the goats on the left. 34 Then the King will say to those on his right, 'Come, you who are blessed by my Father, inherit the kingdom prepared for you from the foundation of the world. 35 For I was hungry and you gave me

Not a parable.

76

food, I was thirsty and you gave me drink, I was a stranger and you welcomed me, 36 I was naked and you clothed me, I was sick and you visited me, I was in prison and you came to me.' 37 Then the righteous will answer him, saying, 'Lord, when did we see you hungry and feed you, or thirsty and give you drink? 38 And when did we see you a stranger and welcome you, or naked and clothe you? 39 And when did we see you sick or in prison and visit you?' 40 And the King will answer them, 'Truly, I say to you, as you did it to one of the least of these my brothers, you did it to me.'

41 "Then he will say to those on his left, 'Depart from me, you cursed, into the eternal fire prepared for the devil and his angels. 42 For I was hungry and you gave me no food, I was thirsty and you gave me no drink, 43 I was a stranger and you did not welcome me, naked and you did not clothe me, sick and in prison and you did not visit me.' 44 Then they also will answer, saying, 'Lord, when did we see you hungry or thirsty or a stranger or naked or sick or in prison, and did not minister to you?' 45 Then he will answer them, saying, 'Truly, I say to you, as you did not do it to one of the least of these, you did not do it to me.' 46 And these will go away into eternal punishment, but the righteous into eternal life." (Matthew 25:31-46) ESV

In this passage both the righteous and the unrighteous are gathered and the purpose of the judgment is to separate them. The righteous will enter into eternal life and the age to come. The wicked will go away into eternal punishment. If this is the purpose of the judgment, then the judgment of the wicked and the righteous must occur at the same time. If the judgment of the wicked and the righteous occurs at the same time, then premillennialism's assertion that the wicked are judged one thousand years after the saints cannot be true.

The theme of the judgment as separation of the wicked and the righteous occurs throughout Jesus's teaching. In the parable of the weeds, Jesus taught that the angels will pull the weeds out from among the wheat, separating them, and burn the weeds in fire

WEEDS 77

(Matthew 13:40-43). This teaching is reinforced in the parable of the dragnet where sorting and separating the wicked and the righteous comes at the end of time (Matthew 13:47-50).

If the purpose of the judgment is the vindication of God's justice and the sorting and separating of the righteous from the wicked, then the final judgment must include both the judgment of the wicked and the judgment of the righteous. If the judgment of the righteous and the wicked does not occur at the same time, then Jesus's parables were a poor parallel to actual events. Why would the harvest time occur in such a way that all the wheat is pulled from the field and then one thousand years later the weeds are pulled and burned? In that case no sorting is needed. The very act of resurrecting the righteous is a sorting act in and of itself. The same is true of the parable of the net. If the net only draws in the righteous and then one thousand years later draws in the wicked, no sorting is needed.

But the wicked will be sorted from the righteous at the end. They will be evaluated according to their deeds. Those found righteous will enter eternal life with Christ. Those found wicked will endure everlasting punishment.

This teaching is set into focus in a startling and plain passage in the book of Revelation. It's plain because of its language, but also because it is so familiar and so parallel to what comes before. There is no mystery here that must be harmonized with the rest of Scripture. The Great White Throne judgment in Revelation 20:11-15 confirms and is consistent with what has come before.

The White Throne

Then I saw a great white throne and him who was seated on it. From his presence earth and sky fled away, and no place was found for them. And I saw the dead, great and small, standing before the throne, and books were

78

opened. Then another book was opened, which is the book of life. And the dead were judged by what was written in the books, according to what they had done. And the sea gave up the dead who were in it, Death and Hades gave up the dead who were in them, and they were judged, each one of them, according to what they had done. Then Death and Hades were thrown into the lake of fire. This is the second death, the lake of fire. And if anyone's name was not found written in the book of life, he was thrown into the lake of fire. (Revelation 20:11-15) ESV

Christ will judge all of the dead before his throne. He will judge them according to their deeds. This judgment is after the resurrection and includes those living on the earth at the return of Christ and those who died before Christ's return. Death and Hades, the place of the dead, will be destroyed. The wicked will be judged by being thrown into Hell, the lake of fire.

The judgment seat of Christ may raise concerns for each of us, and even insecurity. We know that our works do not measure up. How can we enter into salvation if Jesus will judge us by our works? There are whole books on that subject alone. Judgment according to works does not conflict with salvation by faith alone through grace alone. We are saved by faith, not by anything that we have done. Our works confirm our faith. Our life lived is our faith revealed.

Jesus will look at my works. My sins will be paid for by His blood, and every good work will be the product of His grace. I will enter the joy of the Lord and the reward of the Father even if my only good work was to believe in Christ (John 6:29).

Jesus will judge us by our works, but never outside of the context of grace and what He has done. We are in Him. He has given us His righteousness, and that gift has produced righteous works of faith that bring glory to God.

May we live with the judgment seat of Christ in our spiritual vision, and may we have a strong hold on these truths as we approach the book of Revelation in the next chapter.

CHAPTER 15: INTERPRETING THE BOOK OF REVELATION

Have you read John Darby and studied the end times?"
I don't remember my response, but my Syrian friend continued to zealously explain the importance of dispensational eschatology and urged us to use this Bible study to examine the book of Revelation. We were meeting in a coffee shop in a neighborhood populated by immigrants from a different religious background. Our Bible study included me and a friend who were reaching out to immigrants in the neighborhood, our Syrian friend who we hoped would begin to labor and proclaim the Gospel to his Arab neighbors, and an Albanian friend who had been off of heroin for a few months.

Dispensational eschatology and the book of Revelation were pretty low on my priorities list for that Bible study. The book of Revelation would still be low on my priorities for that Bible Study, but I do believe that the book of Revelation can be understood and can be edifying for every single believer, including someone who has just come to Christ.

The book of Revelation has been mysterious from the time it was written. Interpreters agree that it is highly apocalyptic and symbolic. Many of these symbols seem difficult to understand. Revelation is undoubtedly rich with secrets to discover. But I am convinced that every believer can understand the message of the book of Revelation.

Revelation is explicitly about Jesus. It reveals truth about the end times, but the book of Revelation claims that it reveals Christ—not the apocalypse (Revelation 1:1–3).

The best way to understand the book of Revelation is with the same principles we have used in the rest of this book. Start with the big picture. Try to understand the clear, general teaching of the book, and then move into the details. The details are important, but we can't let them confuse the big picture.

Warfare

The general message of the book of Revelation is the supremacy of Christ, His warnings to His church, and the revelation of spiritual warfare that will culminate at the end of time. Satan wars against the church by trying to counterfeit God's plan. God created Adam in his image (Genesis 1:27). Satan enticed Adam into corruption through sin. God sent his perfect imager in Christ (Colossians 1:15). Satan counterfeits a beast in his image (Revelation 13:1). Jesus sends the Holy Spirit to empower His church. Satan counterfeits a "False prophet" to work miraculous signs to deceive the church (Revelation 16:13, 13:13).[9] God readies his bride for the wedding supper of the Lamb. Satan counterfeits a false church and spreads it through the earth. While God prepares a bride, Satan prepares a prostitute (Revelation 17–18). Satan wars on the saints using his counterfeits to both persecute and seduce.

---

[9] Poythress, V. (2000). The returning king. Phillipsburg, NJ. P&R Publishing. "Counterfeiting."

Interpretation

Remember the different schools of interpretation we introduced in Chapter One? If not, go and review them quickly. I like to say that I am a partial preterist, partial historicist, partial futurist, idealist. That's a bit of a joke, but there are important truths in each school of interpretation and much truth when we combine them.

You can claim to be a partial preterist if you believe that the book of Revelation meant something to its initial audience. The first century church found Revelation relevant and urgent to their lives. 70 AD does represent a fulfillment of Bible prophecy. They did go through tribulation, and they did experience the persecution of an antichrist (1 John 2:18). However, I don't believe that this was the only fulfillment of those prophecies.

You can be a partial historicist if you believe that Revelation does describe patterns of spiritual warfare through history. There is a reason believers in history identified Napoleon, Hitler, and Stalin as the antichrist. There is a reason we can always find connections to the book of Revelation in the news. Satan is warring against God's church. Satan does not know when the end will occur. He strains against his bonds trying to bring about antichrists and tribulations in every generation.

You can be a partial futurist if you believe the book of Revelation describes what will happen in the future. Those prophecies are for us. We can look forward to tribulation and Christ's return. What the book of Revelation describes will continue to occur in the future until the end of this age.

You can identify as an idealist if you view the book of Revelation as primarily symbolic of patterns of spiritual warfare throughout history. Revelation's words and their fulfillments have been occurring from the time Christ rose from the dead and will continue to occur until the final crisis and the return of Christ.

There are so many more things that we could discuss, but for more you really should check out Verne Poythress's study *The Returning King*. We do need to introduce one more idea before we dive in though.

Recapitulation

The book of Revelation does not unfold in chronological order. Like many of the Old Testament prophetic books, John's visions present the same or similar truths from different vantage points. Just because one image or vision occurs before another in the text does not mean it occurs before the other in a timeline. For example, if Revelation goes in a linear order how can all of the wicked on the earth be slain in Revelation 19 and then rebel in Rev 20? This isn't a contradiction in the text. Revelation 19 describes the return of Christ from one vantage point. Revelation 20 zooms out and describes the return of Christ and the end from a broader view. Revelation 19 occurs within the timeline of what Revelation 20 describes.

If you keep your mind on the major themes and the big picture, you won't be confused, you will see Jesus in the Scripture, and you will be encouraged by the God's potent description of His victory on behalf of his church. With these things in mind, let's dive into the hotly debated chapter of Revelation 20.

CHAPTER 16:
REVELATION 20 & 2
THESSALONIANS 2:8-12

N ow that we have looked at the Bible's more basic and clear teaching about the end times it's time to move on to some of the more difficult key passages. Revelation 20 may be the most controversial and most debated of those key passages. Revelation 20 features the only mention of 1000 years associated with Christ's reign. This makes it the focal point for the debate about the millennial reign.

As I've already outlined, I think the Bible's basic teaching on the end times is not and cannot be consistent with a one-thousand-year reign of Christ on the earth after the second coming and resurrection. But that does not mean that I don't believe that Christ will reign in His Kingdom on the earth. It also doesn't mean that I don't believe that Christ Himself will physically reign on the earth. I do—in the New Heavens and the New Earth. What Revelation 20 teaches, is something different.

We should start by looking at the context of Revelation 20. Revelation 19 features a harrowing description of the wrath of the Lamb. Jesus returns to conquer His enemies. In fact, it describes the destruction of all the wicked on the earth at that time. Christ's destruction of His enemy is complete. If Revelation 20 describes events that chronologically follow Revelation 19, then we would expect all of Christ's enemies on the earth to be dead.

Instead, I would argue that Revelation Chapter 20 reiterates the global events of the end. John was not given a set of visions in chronological order showing cascading events. Instead, he was given multiple visions of the same global events. Revelation 20 is a big picture view of the end. The events of Revelation 19 don't precede the events of Revelation 20. They can be found inside the events of Revelation 20.

The Binding and Release

Then I saw an angel coming down from heaven, holding in his hand the key to the bottomless pit and a great chain. 2 And he seized the dragon, that ancient serpent, who is the devil and Satan, and bound him for a thousand years, 3 and threw him into the pit, and shut it and sealed it over him, so that he might not deceive the nations any longer, until the thousand years were ended. After that he must be released for a little while. (Revelation 20:1-3) ESV

John separates this vision from the previous vision in Revelation 19 with the words "Then I saw." This vision contains symbols. We understand that Satan is a spiritual being not just a physical dragon, and that though he is literally bound, it is not a physical chain and a physical pit that contain him. These are visionary symbols the Spirit uses to relate spiritual realities. Within this context it is also reasonable to assume that the thousand years is also symbolic. Numbers in Revelation are rich with meaning and often reflect spiritual reality rather than a specific code of literal fulfillments.

"One thousand years" communicates an expansive amount of time with a definite end.

Along with a vision of the binding of Satan, we also are told the purpose for the binding of Satan, "that he might not deceive the nations any longer, until the thousand years were ended." We understand that Satan would be specifically bound from a specific activity on the earth, deceiving the nations, for an expansive but definite amount of time. After this amount of time, he will be released to perform a specific activity—deceive the nations into attacking the church.

This binding of Satan would not come as a surprise to John. Jesus had already taught His disciples about it:

---

28 But if it is by the Spirit of God that I cast out demons, then the kingdom of God has come upon you. 29 Or how can someone enter a strong man's house and plunder his goods, unless he first binds the strong man? Then indeed he may plunder his house. (Matthew 12:28-29) ESV (see also Luke 10:17-19, Col 2:15, Heb 2:14, 1 John 3:8).

The Reign

---

4 Then I saw thrones, and seated on them were those to whom the authority to judge was committed. Also I saw the souls of those who had been beheaded for the testimony of Jesus and for the word of God, and those who had not worshiped the beast or its image and had not received its mark on their foreheads or their hands. They came to life and reigned with Christ for a thousand years. 5 The rest of the dead did not come to life until the thousand years were ended. This is the first resurrection. 6 Blessed and holy is the one who shares in the first resurrection! Over such the second death

has no power, but they will be priests of God and of Christ, and they will reign with him for a thousand years. (Revelation 20:4-6) ESV

The subject of the vision shifts from the angel and the binding of Satan to thrones where saints who had been martyred and refused to bow to Satan rule with Christ in heaven. In this vision, the dead are resurrected and come to life to reign with Christ. John calls this the "first resurrection," but this is not the resurrection of all men, that will occur after the one thousand years. We already know from the passages we looked at before that the resurrection of all men will occur at the return of Christ and precede the judgment. Does this passage overturn all those passages? Will Christ resurrect some people to live on the earth with Him for one thousand years before He returns to destroy His enemies? Or is there a better explanation?

Scholars debate the meaning of "the first resurrection," but the Bible's previous teaching about the resurrection and the second coming instruct us that this is not the physical resurrection that occurs at the end of time, but a spiritual resurrection. This could be the spiritual resurrection that occurs when believers put their faith in Jesus, which would be consistent with John's writing in His Gospel account (John 5:25). Or it could be the resurrection or waking up of the dead in heaven before the end of time—an intermediate state. There is a lot to study here, but either or both explanations make more sense than a physical resurrection on earth.

We know that the saints rule with Christ now, and that we also will in the future. While the issue is debated among theologians, many Christians already believe that their loved ones are in Heaven with Christ now and have truly "come alive" in a spiritual state.[10]

---

[10] Others believe that those who have died "sleep" or exist in state of unconsciousness while they await the final resurrection of the dead. For more on the intermediate state you can check out Anthony Hoekema's *The Bible and the Future* or a systematic theology text like Wayne Grudem's.

They await the resurrection of their physical bodies. If this is the case, then physical resurrection is truly the second resurrection. The first resurrection is the spiritual resurrection and eternal life we find with Christ in heavenly places now.

Right now, the saints who have died reign with Christ in heaven while they await the resurrection of their physical bodies. This wait is an expansive amount of time, but it will have a definite end when Christ returns.

---

7 And when the thousand years are ended, Satan will be released from his prison 8 and will come out to deceive the nations that are at the four corners of the earth, Gog and Magog, to gather them for battle; their number is like the sand of the sea. 9 And they marched up over the broad plain of the earth and surrounded the camp of the saints and the beloved city, but fire came down from heaven and consumed them, (Revelation 20:7-9) ESV

Satan is bound now, but he will be released later to deceive the nations again. And what will he deceive them into doing? Will he deceive them into being greedy? Lusting? False religion?

The specific deception which he was bound from doing becomes his priority upon his release. He will deceive the nations from the four corners of the earth into attacking the church. This will result in a final battle which has popularly become known as battle of Armageddon (this name comes from the Greek term in Revelation 16:16). Satan will deceive the nations and bring about a rebellion against the Church.

While much has been made of the names "Gog and Magog," Gog and Magog do not represent Russia or Iran or Turkey. The passage tells us what Gog and Magog are—they are the nations that are at the "four corners of the earth," we would use the phrase "nations from around the globe." They are all of God's enemies. Russia, Iran, and Turkey do not exist at all four corners of the earth. Ezekiel's prophecy confirms this, and points to Gog and Magog as both global and spiritual (Ezekiel 38-39). They are "nations" or rebellious spirits in spiritual realms that parallel rebellious nations. There is no linguistic or historical evidence that Gog and Magog are Russia or Iran.[11]

Satan has been trying to destroy the people of God since the beginning of time. He has waged war in the spiritual realm against humanity since the fall of man. But he also waged war against the people of God in the physical realm as well. The Old Testament is full of stories of war between the people of God and the nations of the earth who were intent on wiping them out. This was the plan of Satan for much of the Old Testament. He intended to destroy God's chosen people through physical warfare, to deceive the nations into attacking the people of God.

Satan's plan failed every time, but he continued to try with massive battles, bloodshed, and miraculous victory for God's people as the result. In fact, God used warfare to judge the nations. Satan's plan backfired, and God used the physical violence of those wars to display His wrath against sin and put a stop to the escalation of violence and corruption.

When Christ came, God put an end to those national wars. He extended His grace through the Gospel of Christ and no longer allowed the nations to be manipulated by Satan into waging global war on the people of God. Instead, he brought the Gospel into the world and commissioned His people to spread it to all nations. Christ reigns in the hearts of His church and is spreading His reign throughout the earth. Satan is powerless to stop this spread through physical violence, and Christ will spread His reign to every nation, tribe, and language.

---

[11] Heiser, M. (2015). The unseen realm. Bellingham, WA. Lexham Press. 364.

But God's judgment will come again. At the end of "this age" and before the age to come, Satan will be loosed to deceive the nations again and manipulate them into waging a physical war against believers (Revelation 20:3). The resulting war and the resulting victory of Christ will reveal the wrath of the lamb and will be God's final victory on earth before the judgment of the living and the dead. Satan, his false prophet, and all who worked for him will be thrown into eternal punishment, and Christ the conquering King will judge the nations before his throne (Revelation 20:10-15).

2 Thessalonians 2:7-12

This understanding of Revelation 20:1-15 is not the only place the Bible describes end times events this way. 2 Thessalonians 2:7-12 parallels this description of end times events.

---

7 For the mystery of lawlessness is already at work. Only he who now restrains it will do so until he is out of the way. 8 And then the lawless one will be revealed, whom the Lord Jesus will kill with the breath of his mouth and bring to nothing by the appearance of his coming. 9 The coming of the lawless one is by the activity of Satan with all power and false signs and wonders, 10 and with all wicked deception for those who are perishing, because they refused to love the truth and so be saved. 11 Therefore God sends them a strong delusion, so that they may believe what is false, 12 in order that all may be condemned who did not believe the truth but had pleasure in unrighteousness. 2 Thessalonians 2:7-12) ESV

Satan is restrained (bound) now but will be revealed (released) in the future to deceive the nations and bring about the final rebellion and judgment. Satan is currently restrained. But the restrainer is removed shortly before Christ returns, revealing the lawless one who deceives the nations. This results in the lost being deceived into rebellion. They will be judged with the lawless one at the return of Christ.

This fits with the description of Satan being bound in Revelation 20.

Revelation 20	2 Thessalonians 2
Satan is bound.	Lawlessness is restrained.
Satan is released.	The restrainer is removed.
Satan deceives the nations into waging war on the saints.	The lawless one deceives the nations with signs and wonders.
Christ returns to judge Satan and the nations	Christ returns to judge the lawless one and the wicked who believed him.

These two passages were written by two different authors with two different revelations. They use different vocabulary, and they mention different perspectives, but the events they describe parallel one another. They describe the Satan's activity before the return of Christ, the resulting rebellion, and the coming judgment before the end.

This may seem complex now, but what John's revelation and Paul's epistle teach us is actually very simple.

- Satan is bound from deceiving the nations (more on this in the next chapter).
- Christ reigns on the earth through His church.
- His church spreads His reign through the gospel.
- Before the end, Satan is released to deceive the nations into waging war on the church.
- The nations unite to wage a physical war on the saints.
- Christ returns and pours out his wrath.

When we combine this with what we have learned so far, we can add a few more points to our recap.

- Christ raises the dead.
- Christ separates the wicked from the righteous at the judgment.
- The wicked go into eternal punishment.
- The righteous go into eternal life.
- The earth is destroyed.
- God makes a new heavens and a new earth where we reign with Him forever.

We can represent these truths on a simple timeline.

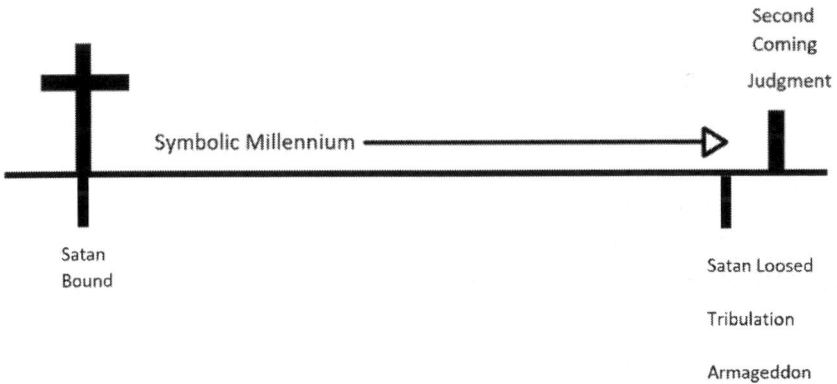

We made it. You now have the full picture. But you may have more questions. In the next chapter we will address the most common question I receive after presenting this simple interpretation of Revelation 20 and the timeline.

CHAPTER 17: SATAN BOUND

"He's saying that Satan is in the season of being bound at present and not deceiving the nations at this time and waging war against the church????? If he's already bound why is there so much evil in the world and why is the apostate church arising??"

Every time I teach on Revelation 20:1-10 the biggest obstacle is helping people understand the binding of Satan. It feels confusing to teach that Satan is bound when we see so much evil in the world. The commenter above is correct: the church is under attack. Believers around the globe are going through some of the most intense tribulations imaginable. Evil abounds. In what way is Satan bound?

As I mentioned in the previous chapter, you must read the binding of Satan in context. Satan is bound from a specific action. He will not be able to unite the nations into a full-scale war on believers until the end. But there is more to the binding of Satan that was important to Jesus and is important to our everyday lives as believers.

---

28 But if it is by the Spirit of God that I cast out demons, then the kingdom of God has come upon you. 29 Or how can someone enter a strong man's house and plunder his goods, unless he first binds the strong man? Then indeed he may plunder his house. (Matthew 12:28-29) ESV

The Kingdom of God, Christ's Reign, is demonstrated by the rule of demons being overthrown; if demons are cast out Christ's rule has come (v. 28). People have interpreted this passage differently at different times. We tend to read Scripture for an eye towards work we must do. But here Christ describes what He has done. Christ has bound the strong man Satan and now is plundering His house by casting demons out of individuals.

Satan no longer has rights or authority on the earth. King Jesus stripped Him of authority by defeating sin and death in the cross and resurrection. When Christ's reign (the Kingdom) arrives, Satan's rule is overthrown. The Kingdom's arrival means Satan's agents are removed. We cast out demons.

Let's go through some well-known passages and take a look at how they relate to Satan's loss of power and binding.

He has delivered us from the domain of darkness and transferred us to the kingdom of his beloved Son, (Colossians 1:13) ESV

We can now be delivered by Christ. We no longer have to be under Satan's rule, we can be under Christ's rule in Christ's kingdom.

> *17 delivering you from your people and from the Gentiles—to whom I am sending you 18 to open their eyes, so that they may turn from darkness to light and from the power of Satan to God, that they may receive forgiveness of sins and a place among those who are sanctified by faith in me.' (Acts 26:17-18) ESV*

The mission of the gospel is to bring people out from the power of Satan. Satan has been bound, now his house, what he owns, can be plundered. The gospel overcomes Satan's deception. Forgiveness and sanctification overcome to bondage of sin. Sin, deception, condemnation, and lies—the tools of Satan's authority—are broken.

> *18 And Jesus came and said to them, "All authority in heaven and on earth has been given to me. 19 Go therefore and make disciples of all nations, baptizing them in the name of the Father and of the Son and of the Holy Spirit, (Matthew 28:18-20) ESV*

Jesus has all authority. Satan has no authority. Jesus has deputized us to assert His rule throughout the nations.

> *17 The seventy-two returned with joy, saying, "Lord, even the demons are subject to us in your name!" 18 And he said to them, "I saw Satan fall like lightning from heaven. 19 Behold, I have given you authority to tread on serpents and scorpions, and over all the power of the enemy, and nothing shall hurt you. (Luke 10:17-19) ESV*

Even before the cross, Christ made his authority apparent. His name on the lips of the disciples was enough to drive out demons from their unauthorized place in God's creation. Demons are now subject to believers in the name and authority of Christ.

John 12:31

---

31 Now is the judgment of this world; now will the ruler of this world be cast out. (ESV)

Satan has been cast out of authority. This happened at the time when Christ was on the earth. He was cast out of authority two thousand years ago. At the end of time he will be cast into Hell.

John 16:11

---

11 concerning judgment, because the ruler of this world is judged. (ESV)

Satan was judged and is under judgement now. He has been convicted and stripped of authority.

Colossians 2:15

---

15 He disarmed the rulers and authorities and put them to open shame, by triumphing over them in him. (ESV)

Satan has been disarmed/bound/restrained. We are now in the mopping up stage of the war. We enforce the victory that Christ won, and the authority Christ has by casting out demons and freeing people through the spread of the gospel. This is God's perspective.

We have already won and are taking back the earth from beaten enemy forces.

Christ bound Satan at the start of His ministry, at the cross, and at the resurrection. Satan has been stripped of all authority or legal right over the earth or its people. We now "plunder Satan's house." We kick him out through the authority of Christ and the power of the gospel.

Along with this spiritual warfare and victory on the earth, Satan is also specifically bound from uniting the nations together against the church until right before the end. Regardless of the evil that permeates the world through sin, although Satan and demons still rule many people's lives, Satan has been stripped of authority. Those who believe experience triumph through submitting to the reign of Christ. They spread that triumph to others by spreading Christ's rule. And we will continue to do that until the end, when Satan will unite the world's forces in one final attempt to crush the church. At that darkest moment Christ will return and judge the wicked, vindicate the righteous, and usher in a brand-new world. We will live with Him forever.

This is such good news about God's victory and Christ's triumph over the powers of evil. How can we not be optimistic about the end? In the next chapter we will review some of the sobering teaching about the end and take a look at how sometimes optimism can go too far.

CHAPTER 18:
DIFFERENCES WITH
POSTMILLENNIALISM

Y es!" my friend shouted in response to my explanation of the tribulation. "Partial preterism. Victorious Eschatology," he said. My friend is another church planter who has seen God multiply churches. I believe that one of the reasons for his fruitfulness is his exuberant faith and optimism. I think my friend has a realistic view of the end times, but sometimes our optimism can cause us to overlook some of the Scripture's important warnings about the end.

I do not have the same exegetical and interpretive problems with postmillennialism that I do with premillennialism. Postmillennialism asserts that Christ will return after a 1000-year rule upon the earth which represents the success of the church's mission on the earth.

As I wrote in Chapter One, there are two different approaches within postmillennialism. The revivalist approach believes that the

1000-year reign of Christ represents a time of Christian revival and success in mission that will then usher in the return of Christ. The reconstructionist approach believes that the church's success in mission will result in a theocratic rule. They believe Christians will rule the earth for a literal or figurative 1000-year reign that will usher in the return of Christ.

Both amillennialism and postmillennialism assert that Christ is going to return after the 1000-year reign, and that's why they both avoid some of the problems that premillennialism has. But there are important differences between the two. The first is a technical difference. Amillennialism teaches that Christ is reigning right now and that the millennial reign is right now. Christ has been reigning since his kingdom proclamation that the kingdom was at hand in his ministry. Amillennialism asserts that Satan is bound right now and that we are plundering his house. Amillennialists are not waiting for a certain measure of success for the millennial reign to start or looking forward to a time when the church includes the majority of the earth's population. Amillennialists believe we're in the millennial reign; we are in the reign of Christ as He reigns in people's hearts through the gospel. Postmillennialism asserts that we are waiting for a millennial age of Christian success and prosperity on the earth.

This technical difference leads into a difference of optimism or expectation. Postmillennialists believe that the church is going to succeed in mission to the point that most of the nations will be Christianized before the end. Some believe that this will result in a theocracy.

I do not believe the church should or will ever establish a theocracy. Jesus said in John 18:36 "My kingdom is not of this world if my kingdom were of this world in my servants would be fighting so that I would not be handed over to the Jews but as it is my kingdom is not this realm" (ESV). I don't believe Jesus's kingdom is of this world, and I don't believe it ever will be. I will not spend more time confronting this issue as most postmillennialists do not hold this view.

Back to the Parables

In Matthew 13:18-23 Jesus explains the meaning of the parable of the sower or the parable of the four soils. The seed lands on different soils in the same way that the gospel receives different responses. I believe that the parable of the sower holds up for all time. There will always be a mixed response to the gospel. And I believe the intention of the parable is to teach that as long as we are in this age, we will never enter a time where everyone receives the gospel. There will always be thorns. There will always be birds stealing the seed. There will always be rocky soil. There will always be the sun scorching growth.

Jesus continues to teach the parable of the wheat and the weeds in Matthew 13:24-30. In this parable the wheat and the weeds grow together. At the end the harvesters and separate the wheat from the weeds. The field in this parable is the world, not the church. Jesus says that the people of the Kingdom and the people of the evil one will grow together in the world until the end. They will only be separated at the judgment.

Both the wheat and the weeds will grow together. The wheat (believers) will not eventually choke out the weeds (unbelievers). The weeds will not eventually choke out the wheat. There will be mixture in the kingdom from now until the end. Unbelievers and believers will exist in the world until the very end of time, and then they'll be separated. Postmillennialists argue that eventually the church (the wheat) will take over the world (the field). This parable teaches that the field will contain a mixture until the end.

Matthew 13:31-35 contains the parables of the mustard seed and the yeast, and these parables are optimistic. I believe that we should be optimistic about the church and its mission. The kingdom will grow and spread throughout the earth until it touches every nation. The kingdom will spread throughout the whole world. The gospel of the kingdom will be preached in all the world; disciples will be made of all nations. People from every tribe and people and tongue are going to worship before God's throne. The church's mission will be successful in bringing the gospel to every people, but that does not mean that most of the world will be believers.

Future Trouble

If you hold to a postmillennial view and believe that most of the world will be Christianized, you must take a lot of passages that seem predictive about trouble before the final end and say that they apply only to the first century or to a certain time period.

Now the Spirit expressly says that in later times some will depart from the faith by devoting themselves to deceitful spirits and teachings of demons, 2 through the insincerity of liars whose consciences are seared, 3 who forbid marriage and require abstinence from foods that God created to be received with thanksgiving by those who believe and know the truth. 4 For everything created by God is good, and nothing is to be rejected if it is received with thanksgiving, 5 for it is made holy by the word of God and prayer. (1 Timothy 4:1-5) ESV

Paul writes about heresy present in the last days. I do believe this refers to first century heresy and apostasy, but I also believe that it refers to future heresy and apostasy. I do not see this only as present in our time now but also at the final rebellion. This prophecy was true in the first century, is true now, and will be true at the end. There will not be a time in this age when this apostasy does not occur, nor do I think we should relegate this prophecy to only talking about the final rebellion right before Christ returns.

But understand this, that in the last days there will come times of difficulty. 2 For people will be lovers of self, lovers of money, proud, arrogant, abusive, disobedient to their parents, ungrateful, unholy, 3 heartless, unappeasable, slanderous, without self-control, brutal, not loving good, 4 treacherous, reckless, swollen with conceit, lovers of pleasure rather than lovers of God, 5 having the appearance of godliness, but denying its power. Avoid such people. 6 For among them are those who creep into households and capture weak women, burdened with sins and led astray by various passions, 7 always learning and never able to arrive at a knowledge of the truth. 8 Just as Jannes and Jambres opposed Moses, so these men also oppose the truth, men corrupted in mind and disqualified regarding the faith. 9 But they will not get very far, for their folly will be plain to all, as was that of those two men. (2 Timothy 3:1-9) ESV

Paul goes on to describe the times of difficulty at the end further. Paul was warning Timothy because this was present in the first century, but Paul is also predicting this this is something that will occur throughout history until the end. In 2nd Timothy 3:12 Paul wrote that all who desire to live godly in Christ Jesus will be persecuted. Persecution of the church existed in the first century and will exist throughout history until the end. There will never be a time when the church is not persecuted. Persecution will always happen, and I believe that the "all" in 3:12 refers to everybody. Those of us who do not seem to be experiencing persecution in the same way as other parts of the world need to ask ourselves certain questions.

Paul warned Timothy that evil was going to grow worse, and I don't believe he just meant in the first century. There will be a growth of evil until the end. The church will grow like wheat, but evil will grow like weeds. They will grow in quality and quantity together until God separates the wicked from the righteous at the judgment.

Revelation

Postmillennialism requires that you hold a partial preterist view of the book of Revelation and Bible prophecy. While postmillennial scholars like Kenneth Gentry have done an excellent job of showing how the symbolism of Revelation related to first century life and events, they restrict those passages' meaning to the first century. They claim those prophecies are history to us.

Postmillennialists believe the tribulation is over. I believe that there are believers who are undergoing the tribulation right now and that believers will undergo tribulation at the very end. Postmillennialists believe that Babylon has already been judged. I believe that the apostate church and Babylon will persist, will grow, and will continue to experience judgment until the very end. Postmillennialism takes the urgency out of many of Scripture's warnings about the end.

Jesus's Warnings

Jesus warned that many who claim to be believers will not be ready at the end. Many will not be believers at the time; they will be deceived. If the church has mainly gained success in the world and most of the world are genuine believers why would Jesus give these warnings? I believe these warnings are for us, and that we are to steward our oil until the Son of Man returns. We are to be prepared for the coming of the bridegroom, and we are to have faith on the earth during trouble.

When the Son of Man comes, will he find faith on the earth? (see Luke 18:8).

CHAPTER 19: HASTE THE DAY

And Lord, haste the day when the faith shall be sight,
The clouds be rolled back as a scroll;
The trump shall resound, and the Lord shall descend,
Even so, it is well with my soul.[12]

T he famous hymn "It is Well with My Soul" captures the longing all believers should have for the return of Christ when justice will be done and we will enter into the joy of the Lord forever. The hymn's sentiments are perfect, but though the term "haste the day" comes from Scripture, 2 Peter 3:12 uses it differently than the hymn writer.

According to 2 Peter 3:9 Christ has not returned yet because He is patiently waiting for men to come to repentance. God looks into the future and yearns for people from every tribe and nation and language. He waits for the spread of the gospel, unwilling to execute final justice until mercy has spread through more of his creation.

---

[12] Spafford, H. (1873). It is well with my soul [lyrics]. Retrieved from https://library.timelesstruths.org/music/It_Is_Well_with_My_Soul/

Since all these things are thus to be dissolved, what sort of people ought you to be in lives of holiness and godliness, 12 waiting for and hastening the coming of the day of God, because of which the heavens will be set on fire and dissolved, and the heavenly bodies will melt as they burn! 13 But according to his promise we are waiting for new heavens and a new earth in which righteousness dwells. (2 Peter 3:11-23) ESV

Peter's letter tells us to wait for the coming day of God, and to "hasten" it by living in holiness and godliness and by fulfilling God's desire to pursue eternal things. We must declare the Good News of Christ's Kingdom that Jesus may receive the reward of His suffering and that the Father may receive His desire. Jesus purchased the lives of men and women on the cross, and today His grace is reaching out through His church to seek and to save the lost. We must not wait quietly for the end to come. We must hasten that day with the bold and constant proclamation of the gospel.

By the grace of God, I live in a community of believers where we make it our aim to share the gospel many times per week with those who have never heard. I wanted to be this kind of person from the day I came to know Jesus, but it took years of growth and the help of many godly leaders and family to help me become that person. May God transform us into people zealously proclaiming Christ's reign until His return.[13]

Christ is coming soon. Today is the day to plunder Satan's house and set the captives free.

---

[13] If you want help becoming someone who proclaims the gospel as part of your lifestyle, you can contact me through the information at the back of this book.

Christ is coming soon. Today is the day to purge the leaven—the sin—from your house.

Christ is coming soon. Today is the day to leave Babylon—this world's sinful system—and live as a pilgrim on the earth.

Christ is coming soon. Today is the day to invest in the eternal—the Word of God and the souls of man.

Christ is coming soon. Today is the day to prepare to enter the kingdom through tribulations (Acts 14:22).

Christ is coming soon. Today is the day to go and buy oil for your lamp before it is too late. Exchange what this world values and invest in an intimate and passionate relationship with Jesus the Messiah that will last forever.

This age is coming to an end. Jesus will return. Those who have died in Christ will rise and meet him in the air. He will execute judgment on His enemies on the earth. This world and everything in it will be destroyed by fire. Christ will separate the wicked from the righteous. The wicked will go into eternal punishment. The righteous will enter into the joy and rest of the Lord in the New Heavens and the New Earth.

Therefore, beloved, since you are waiting for these, be diligent to be found by him without spot or blemish, and at peace. [. . . .] 17 You therefore, beloved, knowing this beforehand, take care that you are not carried away with the error of lawless people and lose your own stability. 18 But grow in the grace and knowledge of our Lord and Savior Jesus Christ. To him be the glory both now and to the day of eternity. Amen. (2 Peter 3:14, 17-18) ESV

APPENDIX: JESUS'S END TIME PROPHECIES

Some of the major passages I did not address in the main text of this book were Jesus's end times prophecies and warnings in Matthew 24, Luke 21, and Mark 13. If you read the rest of the book, I hope I've given you the tools to understand these passages on your own, but if not, let me give you a quick overview of perhaps the most difficult of Jesus's end times prophecies, Matthew 24.

Matthew 24

Jesus begins by predicting that not one stone of the temple would stand on top of another. This prophecy was famously fulfilled in 70AD, and it is in that context that Jesus begins to tell His disciples to prepare for what is to come. In a manner similar to Old Testament prophecy, Jesus starts by describing events that will come soon, the events of 70AD, but then transitions to things that will be fulfilled at the end of the age. Isaiah does this in Isaiah 7, prophesying about events that will occur in King Rizin's reign but then rapidly transitioning to the coming of the Messiah.

While the events of 70AD may mirror the final trouble at the end of the age, I believe verses three through eight refer to the trouble that opens this age following Christ's ministry on the earth. Verses nine through thirteen bridge the trouble of the first century and the trouble that will come at the end of the century, describing events that apply to both periods. Verse fourteen clearly refers to the end of the age.

In verse fourteen Jesus transitions back to the prophecy of Daniel and the events that would occur in 70AD concluding the description of these events in verse 28. Verse 29 to 31 clearly refer to the end of the age. Verse 29 then transitions to the return of Christ, which seems problematic because verse 29 states "immediately after the tribulation of those days." How can the end of the age occur, and the return of Christ occur immediately after the tribulation of 70AD? We must remember Jesus's audience and context. Jesus was a Jew talking to Jewish disciples at the site of Jewish national pride—the temple. For the Jews who sought political victory the tribulation of 70AD would continue until Christ returned (See Luke 21:24).[14] Today, the Jews do not possess the political or geographic power they were promised in the Old Testament. The temple has not been restored. Jerusalem and Israel have never recovered from 70AD, and if I interpret Jesus's words correctly, they won't until Christ returns and brings the New Heavens and the New Earth.

---

[14] Waldron, S. (2009). *More of the end times made simple.* Amityville, NY. Calvary Press.

APPENDIX: WHAT ABOUT DANIEL?

Daniel may be the most complex and difficult of the Old Testament prophetic books. It is certainly one of the most studied and debated subjects in eschatology. I can't solve all of the mysteries of Daniel in this small appendix in the back of this small book but let me give some road signs that I have found useful from my own study.

Daniel's meaning has been hidden until the last days (Daniel 12:4). I believe this means that Daniel, unlike Revelation, was a puzzle and mystery to the people of that time period. It was only until the New Testament came that believers have been able to grapple with Daniel's meaning. I believe that what Daniel conceals, the book of Revelation reveals. We should use the New Testament to interpret Daniel.

Additionally, I believe that we should keep the clear things that the New Testament teaches and use them to interpret Daniel. Any interpretation of Daniel that disagrees with the New Testament's clear teaching should be rejected. This narrows down the possible interpretations.

Daniel features numbers and details and many interpreters present complex and impressive schemes laying out the significance of these dates and numbers. This is especially true of the 70 weeks of Daniel 9:21-27. However, as I have investigated these claims, I do not believe that any such numerical schemes pass deep scrutiny. There are too many problems to interpret Daniel's 70 weeks in a tight time-line. I believe we should take these numbers symbolically. For instance, I see the 70 sevens of Daniel 9:24 not as 490 calendar years but 490 symbolic years pointing to a period of perfect rest in fellowship with God.[15]

This small treatment will hardly satisfy the critic or the debater, but I hope it gives a roadmap for further study.

[15] Poythress, V. (2014). Left Behind? Making Sense of the Days of Daniel [Video Lecture]. Retrieved from https://faculty.wts.edu/lectures/left-behind-making-sense-of-the-days-of-daniel/

APPENDIX: WHAT ABOUT ISRAEL?

A millennialism allows for several views on Israel's role in the end times scheme and the fulfillment of God's promises to Israel. Amillennialism does not allow for a physical reign of Christ on the current earth (but does see Christ reigning on the New Earth), and sees Christ as currently reigning on the throne of David in the heavenly Jerusalem (Acts 13:32-37, Acts 2:29-36). While many views of Israel and the end are compatible with the simple truths I've laid out in this book, the view that Christ will return, rebuild the temple, and receive animal sacrifices again is not compatible with amillennialism. I do not believe that animal sacrifices are compatible with the New Covenant regardless of how one may see Israel's role in the unfolding of the last days.

Some amillennialists believe that God will fulfill all of his promises to Israel through the church. Some believe that God will fulfill the land promises with physical land. Some believe God will fulfill the land promises in the New Heavens and the New Earth. Some amillennialists believe that Romans 9-11 refers to a movement of faith among the Jewish people before the end. Some amillennialists believe that "all Israel will be saved" refers to all who become Israelites through faith (Ephesians 2:11-19. Romans 2:25-29, Galatians 3:16, 26-29).

I personally see Romans 9-11 as referring to ethnic Israel and expect a time of spiritual harvest among the Jewish people before Christ returns. Israel was called to bring the gospel and the Messiah into the world and still has that call. God is not a nationalistic deity. He does not favor one nation or one people group over another. But he does choose different people to have different callings. He chose Abraham and his descendants. He called the nation of Israel to host the arrival of Jesus the Messiah. That calling is irrevocable (Romans 11:29), and I believe that God is still using Israel this way. What that looks like is not always clear.

I believe that God can use current events in this way, but do not await specific fulfillments in the same way that dispensational premillennialists do. Nor do I believe that faith in Christ demands loyalty to Israel as a nation. I suspect that we will best understand the prophecies about Israel after God brings them to pass.

I believe that according to Hebrews 11:10 Abraham looked forward to the New Jerusalem and that God is going to give Abraham's descendants the whole earth through Christ (Psalm 37:11, Matt 5:5, Romans 4:13). We who are gentiles join the originally Jewish church to proclaim the rule of the Messiah throughout the earth, and we take back territory for God and His people through the gospel and in the name of Jesus.

APPENDIX: WHAT ABOUT THE TRIBULATION AND THE ANTI-CHRIST?

The Tribulation and the Anti-Christ are some of the popular topics in end times teaching, yet here I have buried them in the appendix. I hope what I have written about approaching the Scriptures and the book of Revelation will help bring clarity as you study the tribulation and the anti-christ. I believe in both. But I also believe in many of both.

I believe that believers went through the tribulation in 70Ad. I also believe that some believers are going through the tribulation right now. And I believe that believers will endure the tribulation before the return of Christ.

I believe the seven seals, seven trumpets, and seven bowls are symbolic of man's evil and God's judgment throughout history, culminating in the end-times before the return of Christ. I do not see these descriptions in Revelation as literal, but as symbolic of trouble throughout the earth, the same way that the prophets' predictions of Jerusalem's fall contained symbolic language.

I hold similar views about the anti-Christ. I believe Nero was an anti-Christ. I believe there are many anti-Christs already in the world (1 John 2:18), and I believe an anti-Christ will rise before the end of time to unite the nations in attacking the church.

I encourage you to test these concepts out with Scripture. If you would like to do a deeper study on these topics, I recommend *Four Views on the Book of Revelation*, *The Returning King* by Vern Poythress, and *The Triumph of the Lamb* by Dennis Johnson.

APPENDIX: WHAT ABOUT CHURCH HISTORY?

One of the most common arguments made against amillennialism is not a biblical argument, but a historical one. Proponents of premillennialism have argued that the writings of church history and the early church fathers contain no evidence of any end times view other than premillennialism until Augustine (who was amillennial). They argue that any view other than premillennialism is a recent invention and was not part of apostolic teaching that was passed down from Christ and the twelve Apostles.

While this view of the early church fathers is popularly held, it is lacking. A careful examination of the early church fathers reveals that premillennialism was not the only view present in the early church, and evidence suggests that a number of early church fathers were not premillennial.

Charles Hill's study of the millennium in early Christianity identified several early church fathers who were not premillennial. He claims that that Clement of Rome, Ignatius of Antioch, Polycarp of Smyrna, Hermas, the author of 2 Clement (all of whom wrote in the first century) as well as the author of the Epistle to Diognetus and other authors in the second and third century were not premillennial but either postmillennial or amillennial.[16]

Hill's scholarship may be one side of a larger debate on the evidence of early church writings, but Justin Martyr, who was a premillennialist, made a clear statement on the subject. He unambiguously stated that "many" believers during his day were not premillennialists. Stating of premillennialism "many who belong to the pure and pious faith, and are true Christians, think otherwise."[17]

The early writings that we do have are primarily premillennial, but they are not exclusively so, nor do they claim that Christian faith at the time was exclusively premillennial (Justin Martyr claims the opposite). In addition, none of these writings would agree with dispensational premillennialism, but with historic or post-tribulational premillennialism. They also invariably promote some kind of futurist interpretation of biblical prophecy.

While early church writings do not prove a millennial perspective, they are not problematic for amillennialism. Early church writings are however problematic for preterists and partial preterists who deny a future tribulation and some form of antichrist and for dispensationalists who expect a rapture.[18]

---

[16] Hill, C. (2001). Regnum Caelorum: Patterns of Millennial Thought in Early Christianity. Grand Rapids, MI. Eerdmans.

[17] Schaff, P. (1885). The anti-nicene fathers volume 1. Christian Classics Ethereal Library. Retrieved from https://www.ccel.org/ccel/schaff/anf01.viii.iv.lxxx.html

[18] Ladd, G. E. (1956). The blessed hope: a biblical study of the second coming. Grand Rapids, MI. Eerdmans.

SELECTED BIBLIOGRAPHY

Gentry, K. (2014, December 12). JAMES WHITE AND 2 TIMOTHY 3 (2) [Blog post]. Retrieved from (https://postmillennialworldview.com/2014/12/12/james-whites-and-2-timothy-3-2/)

_____. (2014, December 4). END-TIME REVOLT IN DISPENSATIONALISM AND POSTMILLENNIALISM [Blog post]. Retrieved from (https://postmillennialworldview.com/2014/12/03/end-time-revolt-in-dispensationalism-Postmillennialism/?fbclid=IwAR3BzTO9kdRE7sAKiwNXW1_cTlFXjp8Mp7lVzoGnO1CbfTkUJhCpx6Qfsyc#more-5482)

Gundry S. N. and Pate C. M. (1998). Four views on the book of revelation. Grand Rapids, MI. Zondervan.

Heiser, M. (2015). The unseen realm. Bellingham, WA. Lexham Press.

Hoekema, A. (1979). The Bible and the future. Grand Rapids, MI. Eerdmans.

Johnson, D. (2001). Triumph of the lamb: a commentary on Revelation. Phillipsburg, NJ. P&R Publishing.

Kline, M.G. (1974). The covenant of the seventieth week. *The Law and the Prophets: Old Testament Studies in Honor of Oswald T. Allis, 452-469.* Retrieved from (https://www.monergism.com/thethreshold/sdg/Kline,%20Meredith%20-%20The%20Covenant%20of%20the%20Seventieth%20W.pdf)

Lamorak. (2010). Comparison of Christian millennial interpretations [Online image]. Retrieved from URL (https://upload.wikimedia.org/wikipedia/commons/8/89/Millennial_views.svg)

Peterson, R. (2010). Lesson 31 Last Things. Retrieved from (https://itunes.apple.com/us/podcast/spirit-church-last-things-audio-lectures/id418584122?mt=2)

_____. (2010). Lesson 32 Last Things. Retrieved from (https://itunes.apple.com/us/podcast/spirit-church-last-things-audio-lectures/id418584122?mt=2)

_____. (2010). Lesson 33 Last Things. Retrieved from (https://itunes.apple.com/us/podcast/spirit-church-last-things-audio-lectures/id418584122?mt=2)

_____. (2010). Lesson 34 Last Things. Retrieved from (https://itunes.apple.com/us/podcast/spirit-church-last-things-audio-lectures/id418584122?mt=2)

_____. (2010). Lesson 35 Last Things. Retrieved from (https://itunes.apple.com/us/podcast/spirit-church-last-things-audio-lectures/id418584122?mt=2)

_____. (2010). Lesson 36 Last Things. Retrieved from (https://itunes.apple.com/us/podcast/spirit-church-last-things-audio-lectures/id418584122?mt=2)

_____. (2010). Lesson 37 Last Things. Retrieved from (https://itunes.apple.com/us/podcast/spirit-church-last-things-audio-lectures/id418584122?mt=2)

_____. (2010). Lesson 38 Last Things. Retrieved from (https://itunes.apple.com/us/podcast/spirit-church-last-things-audio-lectures/id418584122?mt=2)

Poythress, V. (1985). Hermeneutical factors in determining the beginning of the seventy weeks (Daniel 9:25). *Trinity Journal.* 131-149. Retrieved from (https://frame-poythress.org/hermeneutical-factors-in-determining-the-beginning-of-the-seventy-weeks-daniel-925/)

_____. (2000). The returning king. Phillipsburg, NJ. P&R Publishing.
_____. (2014). Left Behind? Making Sense of the Days of Daniel [Video Lecture]. Retrieved from (https://faculty.wts.edu/lectures/left-behind-making-sense-of-the-days-of-daniel/)

Riddlebarger, K. (2011 10 "The Two Age Model" -- Part 1" [Audio lecture]. Retrieved from

(https://www.monergism.com/legacy/mt/mp3/Amillennialism-101-mp3-series-kim-riddlebarger)

_____. (2011 18 "Signs of the End" [Audio lecture]. Retrieved from (https://www.monergism.com/legacy/mt/mp3/Amillennialism-101-mp3-series-kim-riddlebarger)

_____. (2011). 01 What Is Amillennialism? [Audio lecture]. Retrieved from (https://www.monergism.com/legacy/mt/mp3/Amillennialism-101-mp3-series-kim-riddlebarger)

_____. (2011). 02 Interpreting Bible Prophecy -- Part 1 [Audio lecture]. Retrieved from (https://www.monergism.com/legacy/mt/mp3/Amillennialism-101-mp3-series-kim-riddlebarger)

_____. (2011). 03 "Interpreting Bible Prophecy"—Part 2 [Audio lecture]. Retrieved from (https://www.monergism.com/legacy/mt/mp3/Amillennialism-101-mp3-series-kim-riddlebarger)

_____. (2011). 04 "Covenant Theology and Eschatology" [Audio lecture]. Retrieved from (https://www.monergism.com/legacy/mt/mp3/Amillennialism-101-mp3-series-kim-riddlebarger)

_____. (2011). 05 "These Things Were Foretold" [Audio lecture]. Retrieved from (https://www.monergism.com/legacy/mt/mp3/Amillennialism-101-mp3-series-kim-riddlebarger)

_____. (2011). 06 "These Things Were Foretold" (Part 2) [Audio lecture]. Retrieved from (https://www.monergism.com/legacy/mt/mp3/Amillennialism-101-mp3-series-kim-riddlebarger)

_____. (2011). 07 "The Basic Eschatology of the NT" [Audio lecture]. Retrieved from (https://www.monergism.com/legacy/mt/mp3/Amillennialism-101-mp3-series-kim-riddlebarger)

_____. (2011). 08 "Christ: The True Israel" [Audio lecture]. Retrieved from (https://www.monergism.com/legacy/mt/mp3/Amillennialism-101-mp3-series-kim-riddlebarger)

_____. (2011). 09 "Christ: The True Temple" [Audio lecture]. Retrieved from (https://www.monergism.com/legacy/mt/mp3/Amillennialism-101-mp3-series-kim-riddlebarger)

_____. (2011). 11 "Two Age Model " -- (Part 2) [Audio lecture]. Retrieved from (https://www.monergism.com/legacy/mt/mp3/Amillennialism-101-mp3-series-kim-riddlebarger)

_____. (2011). 12 "Two-Age Model and NT Parallels" [Audio lecture]. Retrieved from (https://www.monergism.com/legacy/mt/mp3/Amillennialism-101-mp3-series-kim-riddlebarger)

_____. (2011). 13 "The Kingdom of God" -- Part 1 [Audio lecture]. Retrieved from (https://www.monergism.com/legacy/mt/mp3/Amillennialism-101-mp3-series-kim-riddlebarger)

_____. (2011). 14 "The Kingdom of God" --Part 2 [Audio lecture]. Retrieved from (https://www.monergism.com/legacy/mt/mp3/Amillennialism-101-mp3-series-kim-riddlebarger)

_____. (2011). 15 " New Creation and the Age of the Spirit" [Audio lecture]. Retrieved from (https://www.monergism.com/legacy/mt/mp3/Amillennialism-101-mp3-series-kim-riddlebarger)

_____. (2011). 16 "The Church as the Israel of God " [Audio lecture]. Retrieved from https://www.monergism.com/legacy/mt/mp3/Amillennialism-101-mp3-series-kim-riddlebarger

_____. (2011). 17 "The Suffering Church" [Audio lecture]. Retrieved from (https://www.monergism.com/legacy/mt/mp3/Amillennialism-101-mp3-series-kim-riddlebarger)

_____. (2011). 19 "Signs of the End" (Part 2) The Antichrist [Audio lecture]. Retrieved from (https://www.monergism.com/legacy/mt/mp3/Amillennialism-101-mp3-series-kim-riddlebarger)

_____. (2011). 20 "The Blessed Hope" (Part One) [Audio lecture]. Retrieved from

(https://www.monergism.com/legacy/mt/mp3/Amillennialism-101-mp3-series-kim-riddlebarger)

_____. (2011). 21 "The Blessed Hope" (Part Two) [Audio lecture]. Retrieved from (https://www.monergism.com/legacy/mt/mp3/Amillennialism-101-mp3-series-kim-riddlebarger)

_____. (2011). 22 "The Rapture" (MP3) [Audio lecture]. Retrieved from (https://www.monergism.com/legacy/mt/mp3/Amillennialism-101-mp3-series-kim-riddlebarger)

_____. (2011). 23 "The Seventy Weeks of Daniel" [Audio lecture]. Retrieved from (https://www.monergism.com/legacy/mt/mp3/Amillennialism-101-mp3-series-kim-riddlebarger)

_____. (2011). 24 "The Olivet Discourse" (Part 1) [Audio lecture]. Retrieved from (https://www.monergism.com/legacy/mt/mp3/Amillennialism-101-mp3-series-kim-riddlebarger)

_____. (2011). 25 "The Olivet Discourse" (Part 2) [Audio lecture]. Retrieved from (https://www.monergism.com/legacy/mt/mp3/Amillennialism-101-mp3-series-kim-riddlebarger)

_____. (2011). 26 "Romans 9-11" (MP3) [Audio lecture]. Retrieved from (https://www.monergism.com/legacy/mt/mp3/Amillennialism-101-mp3-series-kim-riddlebarger)

_____. (2011). 27 "Revelation 20:1-10" (Part One) (MP3) [Audio lecture]. Retrieved from (https://www.monergism.com/legacy/mt/mp3/Amillennialism-101-mp3-series-kim-riddlebarger)

_____. (2011). 28 "Revelation 20:1-10" (Part Two) MP3 (MP3) [Audio lecture]. Retrieved from (https://www.monergism.com/legacy/mt/mp3/Amillennialism-101-mp3-series-kim-riddlebarger)

Storms, S. (2009, October 7). Problems with Premillennialism [Blog post]. Retrieved from (https://www.thegospelcoalition.org/blogs/justin-taylor/what-you-must-believe-if-you-are-a-premillennialist/)

_____. (2013). *Kingdom come: The amillennial alternative.* Fearn: Scotland, UK. Mentor.

Waldron, S. (2003). *The end times made simple.* Amityville, NY. Calvary Press.

_____. (2006). The last things according to peter [Audio lecture]. Retrieved from (https://www.sermonaudio.com/search.asp?subsetitem=Last+Things+According+to+Peter&subsetcat=series&keyword=Sam_E%2E_Waldron&SpeakerOnly=true&includekeywords=&ExactVerse=)

_____. (2009). *More of the end times made simple.* Amityville, NY. Calvary Press.

_____. (2012, February 28). Lecture 1: Eschatology in the Early and Medieval Church [Video lecture]. Retrieved from (https://www.monergism.com/eschatology-comprehensive-historical-and-theological-overview)

_____. (2012, February 28). Lecture 10: The Eschatological Kingdom (Continued) [Video lecture]. Retrieved from (https://www.monergism.com/eschatology-comprehensive-historical-and-theological-overview)

_____. (2012, February 28). Lecture 11: The Intermediate State [Video lecture]. Retrieved from https://www.monergism.com/eschatology-comprehensive-historical-and-theological-overview

_____. (2012, February 28). Lecture 12 [Video lecture]. Retrieved from (https://www.monergism.com/eschatology-comprehensive-historical-and-theological-overview)

_____. (2012, February 28). Lecture 13: The Earthly Prospects & Church/Israel Distinction [Video lecture]. Retrieved from (https://www.monergism.com/eschatology-comprehensive-historical-and-theological-overview)

_____. (2012, February 28). Lecture 14: Pre-Tribulationism [Video lecture]. Retrieved from (https://www.monergism.com/eschatology-comprehensive-historical-and-theological-overview)

_____. (2012, February 28). Lecture 15: Hyper-Preterism [Video lecture]. Retrieved from https://www.monergism.com/eschatology-comprehensive-historical-and-theological-overview

_____. (2012, February 28). Lecture 16: The Final Change & The Eternal State—The Doctrine of Eternal Punishment [Video lecture]. Retrieved from (https://www.monergism.com/eschatology-comprehensive-historical-and-theological-overview)

_____. (2012, February 28). Lecture 17: The Doctrine of the Redeemed Earth [Video lecture]. Retrieved from (https://www.monergism.com/eschatology-comprehensive-historical-and-theological-overview)

_____. (2012, February 28). Lecture 2: Eschatology in the Early and Medieval Church [Video lecture]. Retrieved from (https://www.monergism.com/eschatology-comprehensive-historical-and-theological-overview)

_____. (2012, February 28). Lecture 3: Eschatology in the Reformation and Modern Church [Video lecture]. Retrieved from (https://www.monergism.com/eschatology-comprehensive-historical-and-theological-overview)

_____. (2012, February 28). Lecture 4: The Two Ages [Video lecture]. Retrieved from https://www.monergism.com/eschatology-comprehensive-historical-and-theological-overview

_____. (2012, February 28). Lecture 5: The Two Ages (Continued) [Video lecture]. Retrieved from (https://www.monergism.com/eschatology-comprehensive-historical-and-theological-overview)

_____. (2012, February 28). Lecture 6: The General Judgment [Video lecture]. Retrieved from

(https://www.monergism.com/eschatology-comprehensive-historical-and-theological-overview)

_____. (2012, February 28). Lecture 7: The Eschatological Kingdom [Video lecture]. Retrieved from (https://www.monergism.com/eschatology-comprehensive-historical-and-theological-overview)

_____. (2012, February 28). Lecture 8: The Eschatological Kingdom (Continued) [Video lecture]. Retrieved from (https://www.monergism.com/eschatology-comprehensive-historical-and-theological-overview)

_____. (2012, February 28). Lecture 9: The Eschatological Kingdom (Continued) [Video lecture]. Retrieved from (https://www.monergism.com/eschatology-comprehensive-historical-and-theological-overview)

Welton, J. (2014, April 19). Literal new heavens and new earth? [Blog post]. Retrieved from (https://weltonacademy.com/blogs/jonathanwelton/50140161-literal-new-heaven-and-new-earth)

White, J. (2017). 2 Timothy 3, Amillennialism, Postmillennialism [podcast]. Retrieved from (http://www.aomin.org/aoblog/2014/10/16/2-timothy-3-Amillennialism-Postmillennialism/)

_____. (2017). Resources on eschatology then matt walsh, rome, and mary as mediatrix [podcast]. Retrieved from (http://www.aomin.org/aoblog/2017/04/06/resources-eschatology-matt-walsh-rome-mary-mediatrix/)

FROM THE AUTHOR

I want to thank you so much for reading Prophetic Transformation and spending time with my story. I would love to connect with. You can contact me at JonathanAndTatianaAmmon@gmail.com. I would love to know what you think about the book. You are the reason I am writing, and you are important to me. I also would really appreciate it if you left a review on Amazon or Goodreads.

ABOUT THE AUTHOR

Jonathan Ammon is also the author of *Prophetic Transformation* and a contributor to the *Paid in Full* and *Voice of God* training manuals. His writing focuses on holiness and faithfully hearing and proclaiming God's message. He lives in unusual places and likes to keep a low profile.

Made in the USA
San Bernardino, CA
01 July 2019